"Speaking Your Way to the Top *is a comprehensive, well-written guide for anyone who needs to know how to present themselves effectively in today's marketplace. I highly recommend it!"*

— Tony Alessandra, Ph.D., CSP, CPAE, co-author, *The Platinum Rule*

"This is it! A comprehensive yet thoroughly readable guide for nearly every type of speaker. Great variety, succinct examples, and excellent tip-summaries."

— Margaret Hope, DTM, Toastmasters International Accredited Speaker, President, Lions Gate Training Ltd.

"Marjorie Brody's book provides the core truth and practical skills for achieving powerful communication in every area of your life. These presentation techniques will catapult you forward in your career, your confidence, and your cash flow!"

— Glenna Salsbury, CSP, CPAE, Professional speaker and author of *The Art of the Fresh Start*

"Read this book, apply the principles, and improvement is sure to follow."

— Wayne Choate, DTM, Toastmasters International Accredited Speaker, sales consultant, Asgrow Seed Co.

"Regardless of whether you make presentations for a living, or would rather die than speak before a group, Speaking Your Way to the Top *will help you be a hit with your audiences. Even after 1,000 presentations, I found ideas I put into practice right away. Wish I had something like this years ago when first starting out—it would have made things smoother and easier on the nerves!"*

— Art Sobczak, President, Business By Phone Inc.

"Another masterpiece. Marjorie Brody writes with focus, insight, and passion."

— Tim Connor, CSP, author of the international best-seller, *Soft Sell*

Speaking Your Way to the Top

SPEAKING YOUR WAY TO THE TOP

Making Powerful Business Presentations

MARJORIE BRODY

WILLIAM D. THOMPSON
Series Editor

ALLYN AND BACON

Boston London Toronto Sydney Tokyo Singapore

A Viacom Company
160 Gould Street
Needham Heights, MA 02194

Internet: www.abacon.com
America Online: keyword: College Online

ISBN 0-205-26814-5

Printed in the United States of America
07 08 09 RRD 16 17 18 19 20

**I dedicate this book to the
thousands of "students" I have taught—
both on the college level and in corporations
throughout the world.
Their questions helped me to learn.
Their enthusiasm was an inspiration to me.
Their search for information about selling and
telling in today's marketplace
kept me current and involved.**

**I also want to pay special thanks to
Dr. William Thompson
for his trust in me
and to
Aren Alfaro
for her research and hard work,
which made this book happen.**

Contents

Preface

WHY YOU NEED THIS BOOK

There is an excellent chance that at some point in your business life, you will be making presentations. From going on job interviews to making sales calls, from attending staff meetings to staging full-scale multimedia presentations, the way you present yourself and your thoughts will have a great impact on your career.

Speeches are what most people think of when they hear the word *presentation*. But presentations are much more. They encompass all types of meetings, sales calls, customer service calls, pitches to acquire additional business or new clients, even job interviews. In large companies, hundreds of presentations may take place every day in their various departments and sites. In even the smallest business, there may be two or three: the boss giving a pep talk before the office opens, or just a quick update on a project.

If you are currently working, would like to be working, or are even just thinking about working some day, you have been or will be making business presentations. When you go on a job interview, meet a customer, make a sales call, or give a speech, you are making a business presentation. Whether you are meeting with one person, five people, or a thousand people, you are presenting. If you are at a staff meeting, at a performance evaluation, or selling your idea to a client or boss, you are making a business presentation. In person, on the phone, even on paper, when you communicate about business, you are making a business presentation.

Your purpose will probably fall into one of these categories: to inform, to persuade, or to motivate. Even job interviews fall into these categories, since your objective is probably to inform prospective employers about your qualifications, to persuade them that you are the right person for the job, and to motivate them to hire you. Mastering the skills needed to become a good business presenter will benefit you at the beginning of your career and at every point thereafter: when an employer sees two candidates who have equal qualifications, the better presenter will usually get the job; when two salespeople who have equivalent products make presentations, the one with the superior presentation skills will usually make the sale. Whether you have chosen to work in a high-tech industry, education, healthcare, or customer service, even if you are self-employed, the mastery of good communication skills can mean the difference between success and failure.

It's best to develop an action plan before beginning this program. If you are still in school and beginning your job quest, approach it with the same methods you will use later in your career when developing presentations for meetings or sales calls. If you are already in the business world, select methods that best meet your current career objectives, and save the rest for "what if" situations that may crop up at another time.

As you develop the skills needed to become a good presenter, the feedback you receive from your "audiences" will enable you to judge your progress. Each time you make a presentation, you will be learning and evaluating your progress. Throughout this book, you will find Skill Drills. Do them. They will help you to improve your skills while you are reading this book and later when you are making actual presentations.

1 Understanding the Eight Types of Business Presentations

1. ONE-ON-ONE: INTERPERSONAL COMMUNICATING

Some people would rather present before a large audience than sit down one-on-one with their boss, client, or even job interviewer. When preparing for interpersonal communications, you should put in the same amount of effort as when preparing a more formal presentation. This may be the only opportunity you have to show others who you are and what you have to offer. Use the following steps to guide you through the process:

a. Know how much time is available so you will not have an excessive amount of information to present in a short amount of time. Write your points down ahead of time, including questions you might want to ask (or be asked). Keep to the time schedule; if you find you have interrupted your presentation to answer questions or if the discussion has veered from your topic, mention the points you would still like to cover and find out if there is additional time available to you. If not, offer to complete your presentation at another time.

b. With the exception of a job interview, prepare an agenda. You don't have to give a copy to the person you are meeting with unless it will help him or her follow your points.

c. Be prepared. Gather any research or documents you might need to back up what you have to say. Have a copy ready to present if requested.

d. Practice the points you want to make out loud. This will enable you to hear if what you are saying makes sense. If you can, practice with a partner. Get feedback and adjust your remarks accordingly.

e. If you don't know the answer to a question, say that you'll find out—then do so and respond promptly, either on the phone or in writing.

f. If you are on a job interview, learn as much about the company as you can in advance. Obtain annual reports or company prospectuses; come prepared with comments or questions that show you understand the business and the company. Be prepared to answer the question Why do you want to work for this company? If you are uncomfortable with the interviewing process, or just want to learn more, there are several books available at bookstores or your local library that will help to prepare you. You will be presenting yourself on job interviews, and your resumé, letters of reference, or any other printed materials you will be leaving behind should reflect your professionalism, as should your remarks. Be prepared and practice interviewing skills with friends or others already in the business world.

g. Dress appropriately. Proper business attire is called for even when having a one-on-one meeting. Even if the person you are meeting with is dressed in business casual style, you will look and feel more professional if you are dressed professionally, and that will be reflected in your attitude.

2. GROUP OR STAFF MEETINGS

You are meeting internally with other staff members or you are out of the office at a client meeting. You will be presenting your ideas or sharing opinions in one of two ways: off-the-cuff or with prepared remarks. How you present yourself in these situations can have an important impact on your career. Some ways to present yourself effectively in these situations are:

a. Find out as much as you can about the topic before the meeting and come prepared. If an agenda is available, get a copy in advance. If you are scheduled to comment on a particular subject, knowing in advance will enable you to prepare even if you will not be giving a formal presentation.

At some meetings, topics are assigned to facilitate discussion. You are not expected to be the sole source of information but are expected to lead a discussion. If you are part of a team, decide who will be the overall leader. That person will introduce the topic and the individual participants. The leader will also provide a segue between speakers (if desired) and should assign topic segments in advance. For example, if the topic is the marketing of a new software package, each member of the team may be assigned to discuss one topic, for instance the packaging, timing, the pricing, and so on. Each person may have knowledge of the entire process, but by dividing the topic into segments, each is able to contribute something of value to the discussion. The leader should also make any closing comments and open the floor to questions, which may be answered by the appropriate member of the team (or the one who feels most comfortable answering). The person answering should first paraphrase the question to make sure they have understood it correctly.

b. If you will be making a formal presentation, refer to the later chapter dealing with the specific type of presentation you will be doing.

c. If you will be required only to comment, study the topic that will be discussed so your remarks will be pertinent. Make notes in advance so you will have something to refer back to should you find yourself unable to think of anything new to offer.

d. If you have only a general idea of what will be discussed, try to find out as much information as you can beforehand. If possible, call the person who set up the meeting to find out his or her expectations. Although a formal agenda might not be available, you may get enough information to enable you to contribute something of value. While at the meeting, make points during the discussion to bring attention to your ideas.

e. If you are afraid to speak, write down your comments ahead of time and then, when called upon, refer to your notes as an aid. If you sit silently, you will make an unfavorable impression. At the very least, try to prepare a question or a comment to make at the end.

f. If you are going to a meeting and are unable to learn the topic in advance, you will be at a disadvantage but can still speak up and add to the discussion. Listen to what is said and then agree or disagree as you feel, and tell why.

3. DEPARTMENT OR TEAM MEETINGS

Follow the suggestions given in the preceding section plus the following additions:

a. Find out in advance who will be leading the meeting and meet with him or her either separately or with the rest of the group to discuss his or her expectations and any contributions you might be able to make. Agree on time limits for your part. It is helpful to know who will be presenting both before and after you, and the topics they will be covering. This avoids repetition and ensures that all topics will be presented adequately.

b. Prepare your comments in advance, but be prepared to change them quickly should someone else make the same point. You could just agree with the other person, or add your own insights. Proper advance planning by the team leader should help to avoid this pitfall; however, some overlap may be unavoidable. It also helps to remember that hearing something more than once helps the audience to remember the facts. It may be desirable to have repetition to drive your point home.

The following is an example of an unsuccessful team meeting: A publisher and his staff were interviewing vendors to determine which computer system to use. One vendor invited them to its offices to demonstrate some new technology. The account manager that the publisher had been dealing with told them that she was bringing four other people to the meeting, including experts on publishing and some technical people. The account manager opened the meeting, turned the floor over to the publishing expert, and didn't say another word until the end of the meeting. It was clear from his remarks that the expert had not communicated with the account manager before the meeting because he did not seem to understand the publisher's very specific needs. The publisher's staff were confused when the technical people spoke. After the presentation was over, the account manager apologized for the confusion. She explained that her company had recently instituted a team selling approach and that they hadn't ironed out many of the kinks yet. Needless to say, this company did not get the contract. To work effectively, team selling requires smooth and precise coordination of the entire team, with the prospective client's needs coming first.

10 Tips for Team Leaders

- Prepare with the audience in mind: What are the members expecting to get out of the presentation?
- Have reasonable objectives.
- Arrive early to set up the room, get out materials, and welcome attendees.
- Define objectives, agenda, and ground rules.

- Use a variety of learning opportunities, making the event as experiential as possible.
- Use a variety of learning tools.
- Present information in small chunks giving opportunity for questions.
- Adhere to time constraints.
- Keep things moving.
- Draw conclusions and create action.

4. CLIENT MEETINGS

Client meetings may include meetings set up by the client to learn the status of current projects, to give new assignments to you or your company, or to discuss problems or concerns with existing projects. The client meeting can also be set up by you or another member of your company to solicit new business, to give an update or status report on current business ventures, or to address a problem that has been solved or needs to be solved. Your part in these presentations will dictate what information and how you prepare for the meeting. If you will be responding to questions from your client, the material presented should deal specifically with the request you were given. The meeting should not veer off course without the permission of the person you are meeting. If you have prepared properly, you should be able to anticipate questions and respond properly. If put on the spot and asked for information you do not have, respond honestly—do not attempt to speak about something you don't know. Tell the client or customer that you will find out the information and get back to them. Then make sure you respond promptly.

A client meeting (or a department or team meeting) may demand that you give what is commonly known as an impromptu presentation. Since in most cases you will be speaking about a familiar topic, you will probably just need time to organize your thoughts. Many people find impromptu speaking nerve wracking, but it needn't be if you follow these suggestions:

a. Pause before you begin to speak. This will give you a second or two to organize what you want to say. Start with an opening that gives you some time to think, for example: "You've just asked me to explain why I think sales are down this year. Let me begin by looking at our sales during this last quarter." This has provided you more time to get your thoughts together and to make some good points in the opening and during the speech.

b. Respond to what has already been said. If others have been asked to speak before you, comment on what they said and add to it or give your own take. This is also a chance for you to comment on the audience at large or the topic in general while collecting your thoughts. If you cannot come up with anything new to say, comments on what has already been said should be kept brief. If you are completely stumped, offer to comment later after you have had a few minutes to collect your thoughts.

c. Think positively. Even though you have not had a chance to prepare your remarks, don't refuse to speak. Everyone knows your remarks will be unprepared, so they won't be expecting perfection. If you are uneasy, just give your comments as clearly and simply as possible.

d. Keep it short. Say what you want to say, and then sum up briefly and concisely. This is not the time to ramble on and make everyone sorry you spoke.

e. Present with strength. Even though you are not making a formal presentation, you should be standing, if possible, or else sitting straight up and speaking in an authoritative tone. Make eye contact with others in the room. Pause for emphasis when needed, and increase the volume slightly.

Don't speak exclusively to the person who asked you a question, but address the group at large.

5. SALES PRESENTATIONS

The purpose of a sales presentation may be to acquire a new customer, to generate incremental business from an existing client, to review account activity, or to project sales movement. Sales presentations may even be a regular sales call that takes place the same time every week, month, or year. They can be formal presentations with or without visual aids, or they can be less formal, even one-on-one. They can be meetings with just a few reps or they can involve entire companies. How and what you present will be determined by the meeting format and audience. The larger the audience, the less contact you will have with individual customers. How you present yourself at a formal sales presentation reflects on you and your company and can make or break a client relationship.

As with any presentation, know in advance how much time you will have. If you will be presenting alone, organize your material within these constraints, leaving time at the end for questions. If you will be presenting as part of a group, make sure you are able to complete your part in the time allocated. If you will be using visual aids, make sure the equipment needed is available and appropriate for the meeting room. Proper advance planning and preparation will be critical to your success.

Stick to the topic. Keep in mind the information your audience expects to receive, and make sure you have included it. If you will be bringing bad news, don't mask it; present it in its proper light. If sales are down, you are obligated to report this information. If there is positive news, you should present it after the bad news. If next quarter projections are up, say that after the bad report. If research has come up with some exciting new facts, give those after the bad news. What will be remembered is what comes last. Make sure you have prepared handouts with the highlights of your presentation clearly numbered. Handouts should be easy to read and in keeping with your corporate culture. Now is not the time for cartoons or jokes (unless that's the corporate culture!).

Practice in advance and anticipate the questions you might be asked. Remember, if you don't have an answer, say you'll get the information if the person will meet you after the presentation and give you a phone number or address. Make sure to follow up.

6. CONFERENCE SPEAKING

If you have been invited to speak at a conference, you may already have submitted a brief outline of your topic and key points that you will make. When preparing your presentation, make certain to keep the outline and these key points handy so you won't forget to include them in the final version. Conference speaking can be done as a roundtable discussion, as a more formal speech in front of the room, or as a break-out session. How much time you will have and the preferred format should be determined well in advance of the actual conference.

When preparing your material, keep in mind who will be attending. Focus on meeting the needs of these attendees. For example, if you are a teacher and will be speaking at a conference for other teachers, your material should be fresh, new, and relevant to the particular group. If you have devised a new method of dealing with behavior problems in the classroom but are interested in finding out how other teachers are dealing with this same problem, a roundtable discussion might be the best format. This format will allow you to be the moderator who leads a discussion of the topic and still present your own ideas to the group first.

If you will be leading a break-out session as part of a larger conference, keep in mind that participants may want to discuss material they just heard before hearing what you have to say. Be flexible and ready to change your expectations for the greater good of the group. If, however, you have material that is pertinent to what has just been heard or is necessary for understanding what is yet to come at the conference, lead the session in a direction you think it should take.

7. TEAM PRESENTATIONS

If you are leading a team presentation, it will be your responsibility to organize speakers, to assign the parts, and to oversee all presentations. You will usually be a presenter as well, but as the leader you will be expected to keep things moving before, during, and after the presentations. When determining the parts of a presentation, it is important to keep the following questions and points in mind:

a. How much time do you have for each part?
b. What should be the order of material?
c. Who are the strong/weak presenters?
d. As leader, you should sum up and lead the question-and-answer session.
e. Make sure you have given adequate preparation time for rehearsing and revising.

Pitfalls to Avoid

- Appearing to be disorganized
- Holes in presentation because presenters think someone else is covering the topic
- Poor timing

8. VIDEOCONFERENCES

While telephones, computers, and the written word are still the primary methods of business communication, the video age has taken us much farther in our ability to communicate face-to-face. It is much better to see the person we are dealing with, whether that person is across town or across the globe. With videoconferencing joining the other mainstream methods of communication, we can be face-to-face with anyone, anywhere in the world. Many large corporations now have their own videoconferencing facilities, with an in-house staff to make them work smoothly. But you don't have to work for a large corporation to take advantage of videoconferencing. Many rental facilities exist, staffed by experts who can guide you step-by-step through the process.

The capability of linking two or more locations almost anywhere in the world makes videoconferencing valuable for companies doing business globally. Presenting over a videoconferencing network is very different from presenting to a live audience. Imagine yourself projected onto the screen of your computer. How will you look and how will you sound? You will probably be seated, facing a camera, and a video screen will show the people on the other end of the conference. They will be in a similar set-up. You will probably appear primarily as a talking head. Your visual aids will be presented through another camera, leading to confusion if you have not carefully choreographed with the camera operator when to show them. Find out in advance if you will be able to get up or show the visuals yourself.

When preparing your presentation, keep the camera set-up in mind. If you are unsure of how to prepare, meet in advance with the program facilitator who may be able to show you a sample of an actual videoconference or demonstrate how it will work.

Tips for Videoconferences

- Size counts: videoconferences are best suited to small, geographically disbursed groups; with large groups, it is difficult to see the other participants.
- Have a backup plan if things malfunction. Consider an audio conference if the video fails.
- Make proper introductions. Once connected, let the other site know that you are there. It can be embarrassing to everyone to see and overhear something that was not intended for everyone. As with any meeting, you should be sure that each participant is visible when he or she is introduced.
- Establish a facilitator to run the meeting and make sure the agenda is followed. He or she will also make opening and closing remarks.
- Watch the remote locations. When the room is equipped with monitors for both the remote and the local sites, don't watch yourself on the monitor during the conference. Remember that the other side is watching you: you don't want to be viewed checking your hair or makeup or doing anything unsightly. Focus your attention on the person speaking.
- Pay attention to grooming. The video camera magnifies you. What you wear and how you are groomed is going to be noticed. Visualize yourself projected on a big-screen television; anything out of place is going to show up. Best to avoid checks and plaids and overly bright colors.
- Show consideration for others. Speak in a normal tone of voice; it's not necessary to shout to be

heard. Most videoconferencing systems produce a slight delay of audio between sites. As a result, it is important to wait until the person speaking is finished before commenting. Talking over someone else will cause confusion—and it's rude.

Skill Drill
Don't Be Camera Shy—Tips for When You're Going to Be Videotaped or Videoconferenced

- Prepare a five-minute presentation (subject doesn't matter) and videotape yourself. Watch the tape several times and give yourself an honest critique. Then tape yourself again and do the same thing. If you find that you keep repeating the same mistakes, concentrate on improving them while you videotape yourself again. If you find yourself using power robbers while speaking (*umms, ahs, like, you know*), keep practicing until you can speak smoothly for five minutes without using any. Then videotape yourself again. You may have to do this five or six times before you feel comfortable in front of the camera. If you are unhappy with how you look or your facial expressions, practice speaking in front of a mirror until you have eliminated the unwanted expressions. Then, videotape yourself again.
- If you find yourself terrified of the camera, remember that being comfortable is not something that comes naturally to many people. Even seasoned broadcasters admit to recurring stage fright. A series of relaxation exercises may help you to feel more in

control. Try the ones that follow; you can also use them to relax yourself before presenting, whether on videotape or in front of a live audience.

- If you don't like the way you look on camera, remember that what you have to say is going to be more important than how you look. However, this is the time for a natural hairstyle and natural makeup. Although the lights may make you look washed out, you don't want to look like you're going on the stage. A little more blush for women is usually all that's necessary. For men who perspire and shine when nervous, a light dusting of corn starch applied with a large brush on the nose, forehead, and chin can eliminate that shiny look.
- What you wear can distract from what you have to say. For those on the other end of your videoconference, who may never have seen you before, this is going to be their only impression of you. Choose subdued or neutral colors appropriate to your style and coloring. Men and women should avoid bright, flashy colors and loud ties. Simple jewelry is appropriate; avoid dangling or jangling earrings, bracelets, or necklaces. Men should avoid ties with narrow, repeating stripes, which can be distracting on camera. If you wear glasses, select those with nonglare lenses and rims.

2 Getting to Know Your PAL™ (Purpose, Audience, Logistics)

PURPOSE: TELLING AND SELLING— THREE TYPES OF PURPOSES

Your business presentation will probably fall into one of three types of purposes: **informative**, **persuasive**, or **special occasion**. Unless you are going to focus on a career as a speaker, motivational presentations and those strictly for entertainment are best left to the professionals. As you gain experience as a presenter, you may feel comfortable adding elements from these two categories into your own speeches. Before beginning preparation of your presentation, first decide which type it will be.

The Informative Speech

The informative speech is given to share information with others. Your objective is for the information to be related as clearly and effectively as possible. You want your material to be interesting enough to capture your listener's attention, and you want them to retain the information. Most of the presentations you will give throughout your career will be informative. Delivering an in-house sales update, meeting with your boss or department to review a new product, or talking about your company to prospective employees are all informative presentations—so are training presentations and the committee report you deliver to your local Kiwanis Club.

The Persuasive Speech

The persuasive speech is used to generate action by the audience or to influence behavior. Persuasive speeches can use a logical approach, feeling and emotion, or the speaker's credibility to appeal to an audience. A successful persuasive speech will draw from each of these three approaches in varying degrees, depending on the speaker's style and his or her analysis of the audience. Some situations in which you may find yourself having to be persuasive are

- persuading your boss to give you a raise;
- persuading your bank to give you a loan;
- persuading your team to work longer hours;
- persuading your best employee not to quit;
- persuading your school board to fund a new school; and
- persuading your client not to leave your company.

You may not give many formal persuasive presentations, but you will certainly find yourself in situations in which it is essential to deliver a persuasive presentation in an effective way.

Special Occasion Presentations

At some point in your career, you will probably find yourself in situations falling under the vague heading of "special occasion" presentations. These can be anything from a welcome speech, an introductory speech, an acceptance speech, or an exit speech. They can occur at a retirement dinner, a birthday luncheon, a sports banquet, an award ceremony, the outcome of a project, or the approval of a request. These are presentations that are everyday occurrences for some and occasional events for others.

Once you have determined the type of presentation you will be giving, move onto the next step—identifying whom you will be speaking to.

THE A IN PAL™ REFERS TO YOUR AUDIENCE

Who are they, and what will they expect from you? Before beginning to write your speech, you should spend time developing an audience profile. Because all audiences are different, doing your homework well in advance of your presentation is as important as having well-prepared information. If the audience isn't interested in a specific topic, there is very little you can do to make your presentation work. If you will be speaking about Medicare reform to recent college graduates about to face the job market for the first time, your audience will be less than captive. If, on the other hand, you will be speaking to fellow accountants, attorneys, or teachers, you already have a great deal of information that will make it easier to create your presentation. If you are speaking within your company or industry, you will probably be able to judge whether an audience will be hostile or receptive, depending on the topic: If it's bonuses, you're in luck; if it's downsizing, you may have a difficult time.

When you are able to choose a topic yourself, knowing who composes the audience will let you select a subject that interests as many members as possible. The best source for information about your audience will be the program organizer. You can also ask people you know or get in touch with those who have addressed the same group before. Read literature about the company and any magazine or newspaper articles that might pertain to its corporate culture. It is essential that you do not skip this step when preparing your presentation. Misjudging your audience or not knowing who they are can have disastrous effects on even the best-executed presentation.

Developing the Audience Profile

Before preparing your speech, you will develop an audience profile, including demographics, psychographics, attitudes, learning styles, and identification of the decision makers.

Demographics: What Do You Know about Your Audience?

Demographics include audience characteristics such as age, education, occupation, socioeconomic group, and marital status. These factors will affect the way you use language, the information you choose to include, illustrations and examples, and humor if you are including any. The more details you have about your audience, the less risk there is of offending anyone or of including too little or too much information.

In a business situation, you need to know who will be in your audience. Will officers of the company be there? Will there be many departments, each having its own agenda, or will you be speaking to a narrower base? Will you be speaking to employees at your own level or from different levels? The wider the range in your audience, the more difficult it is to tailor your presentation to meet everyone's needs.

Demographic Audience Profile

When developing an audience profile, include the following demographics:

- Males/females and percentage of each
- Age ranges

- Income levels
- Education levels
- Where do they live?
- Where do they work?
- Married/single/widowed/divorced

Psychographics: What Traits Do They Share?

Identifying your audience's psychographics is the next step. These traits will help you to develop your audience profile further based upon what you can learn about their feelings and impressions of you and your topic.

Psychographic Audience Profile

A psychographic profile should include the following audience data:

- What do they think about your topic? Is it new to them?
- Have they attended any presentations on similar topics?
- What are their hopes, aspirations, dreams, goals?
- What are their interests?
- Are they politically active?
- Have they supported causes like yours before?
- Are they open-minded?

Identifying Decision Makers

Is the company president, your immediate supervisor, or someone you are trying to influence going to be there? Knowing in advance whether decision makers will be in the audience will help you to target your remarks. It will also let you know to whom the audience will be looking for feedback and impressions. Capturing a positive reaction from decision makers in attendance can make your presentation a success even if others in the audience disagree. If you have identified a decision maker in the audience, avoid a common pitfall—addressing your comments to or looking primarily at him or her during the presentation. This could backfire by making the rest of the audience feel less important.

WIIFM: What's In It For Me?

All the members of your audience come to a presentation with agendas of their own, and they want something from the speaker. What they will be looking for from you may be revealed by answers to the following questions:

- What are their experiences with the topic?
- Why are they there? Do they want to be/have to be?
- What do they hope to get out of the presentation?
- What are their trigger issues?
- Are they there with open minds?
- What do they expect from you?

THE L IN PAL™ IS FOR LOGISTICS

A well-prepared speaker has taken the time before presentation day to find out details that can ease tension on the actual speech day. For example, if presenting after lunch, you won't turn the lights out and you won't give a lot of straight lecture—or you may find that your audience falls asleep.

When?

What time will you be presenting? Who speaks before you? After you? How much time will each speaker have? What happens if speakers run over their allotted time limits? Will you be speaking before, during, or after a meal? Will you be speaking first or last?

Where?

Where will you be presenting? You need to know the size of the room, how it will be set up, the available equipment and what you may need to bring, the exact location of the presentation, its correct address (room and floor), and exact directions to the site. Don't forget to find out where the restrooms are so you won't be wandering around looking during the program breaks.

Who?

Who will be there? How many will be there? Who else will be presenting? What will they be speaking about, and for how long? This will help you to avoid the embarrassment of speaking about the same topic; if your topic is the same, you can check with the other speaker to make sure that you are not using the same information. You can also find out if your topic would work better before or after the other speakers have their turns.

How?

How will you be presenting? How much time will you have? How long will there be for questions and answers? Will these be held at the end of each speaker's portion, or will they be at the end of all sessions?

Knowing these details can save you embarrassment and can help you during your program preparations. They can affect many elements of your speech, including the number of handouts you prepare, the size of visuals you will be using, the room set-up, and whether or not you will need to use a microphone. Planning to give a speech to an intimate audience of 20 and finding yourself in front of an audience of 100 can be disconcerting at best and a catastrophe at worst.

3 Organizing Your Presentation

A great deal of work must go into the preparation of any presentation. By taking the time to get organized before you begin to write your presentation, you will save yourself a great deal of anxiety. The 12 steps that follow are an overview of the process you will be using to prepare your presentation. Following them will be a step-by-step guide to developing your own presentations. The chapters that follow on informative and persuasive presentations will further explore the specifics that relate to each.

THE 12 STEPS OF ORGANIZATION

1. Select the Topic

Make sure that it is appropriate for the audience. If it is work related, the topic may have been assigned to you or chosen for you, but you will still follow your PAL™ (Purpose, Audience, Logistics).

2. Limit the Topic to One Central Theme

It is best to say a lot about a little instead of a little about a lot. Limit your topic, keeping in mind the amount of time you have to make your presentation and the level of the audience you will be addressing.

3. Gather the Information

First, write down everything you know about the topic. Then you will be able to evaluate what you need to research and whom you may need to interview or brainstorm with. Remember to include more than just facts and figures—use examples, stories, analogies, case studies, quotes, humor, and the best type of visual aids for your presentation.

4. Choose a Method of Organization

This will depend on the type of presentation you will be giving. (See Chapters 4 and 5.)

5. Outline Your Main Points

Use between three and five main points in the body of your speech to support your central theme. Be sure to add transitions to connect the ideas.

6. Collect Supporting Data

Enhancing key points with interesting secondary information will help your audience to retain the information.

7. Check for Accuracy

Review the previous points to be sure that you have limited your topic and developed the main points. Verify your information.

8. Design the Introduction

Make sure it's catchy and tells the listener WIIFT (What's In It For Them). Include a grabber or hook to get their attention.

9. Write a Strong Conclusion

Refer to your introduction, review key points, or deliver a call to action. Make sure it is memorable.

10. Put Together a Final Draft

Outline your speech on notepaper using large print (avoid index cards). Use only the top two-thirds of each page and leave room in the margins for notes. Use either single words, sentences, or short phrases. Write out your memorable phrases and transitions.

11. Practice Your Presentation

Practice it three to six times out loud. Say it differently each time to keep the spontaneity. Tape record your practice and make any necessary changes.

12. Practice Your Presentation Again and Again

Practice it until you feel it's perfect. Practice does not make perfect. Perfect practice makes perfect.

YOU'RE READY TO BEGIN

The Outline

Your presentation's outline will ensure that you won't leave anything out. It is a planning tool that, used properly, will give shape and form to your presentation. Whether your objective is to inform, persuade, or entertain, whether you will be speaking at a board meeting or a retirement dinner, the outline will guide you through the process of developing an effective presentation.

I recommend using $8\frac{1}{2}$-by-11-inch paper rather than index cards, since note cards can easily get out of order. Outline your speech instead of writing it out word for word. This will give you the freedom to make changes as you go along. The preferred method of outlining is the phrase outline, or short sentence, method. Phrases are long enough to remind you of what you want to say and short enough so your attention will be on the audience and not on the outline. Most points will be written as phrases. The opening and closing can be written out, yet practiced enough so that they are not read.

Transitions will play a crucial role in your presentation. They are necessary to prevent gaps between you and your listeners. You will use transition sentences between your review of your main points and your final, memorable statement. It is acceptable to write out your transitions, any facts or numbers that you need to remember, or other important statements that must be spoken accurately. The following example uses mostly phrases and is organized into an introduction, a body with three main points, and a conclusion. The audience and the purpose of the presentation are listed at the top.

Sample Speech Outline

Audience: Company officers

Purpose: After hearing my speech, the audience will agree that switching to PCs from Macs will be worth any additional cost or retraining.

I. Introduction (grabber, WIIFT, source credibility, and preview)

A. Would you stay with a Mac if you knew it was costing the company more than $500,000 per year in lost sales?

B. As a company dealing in sales, we need to be current and technologically compatible with our customers.

C. As someone who has worked with both Macs and PCs, I know how much the new PC Windows NT software could save us in manpower and could help us achieve increased sales.

D. Switching to PCs can do this.

II. Body

A. There isn't any Mac software that can give us the sales force support we need.

1. Our sales force spends on average 10 hours per week per person on needless paperwork.
2. Our customers are already using Windows NT. Our current equipment and the lack of compatible software are liabilities.
3. We don't know how many of our competitors are already using Windows NT, but some of our customers have already complained that we are not up to date.

Transition: Now that we realize our customers are using PCs, and our competition may be using them, let's look at the benefits of switching.

B. Here are the benefits of switching:

1. Our sales force will have more time to sell—hours spent on paperwork can be used for sales calls and lead generation.
2. Our customers can communicate their reorders directly to the PCs—something they cannot presently do to our Macs.
3. Increased sales are projected at $500,000 while initial cost outlay for new equipment only $50,000.
   a. Hardware—$30,000
   b. Software—$10,000
   c. Retraining—$10,000

Transition: We know that we need to be responsive to our customers' needs and to the needs of our own sales force. Changing to PCs will meet both of these objectives.

C. Our cost of doing business will go down; our efficiency will go up.

1. PC software less expensive than Mac and more current.
2. Will be able to work faster; programs are easier to use.
3. No downside.

III. Conclusion (review and memorable statement)

A. Changing from Macs to PCs will enable our company to enjoy increased productivity, better customer relations, improved job performance, higher sales.

B. Changing to PCs will benefit everyone in the company. Please vote "yes" for this change. I have a computer consultant available to work with us as soon as I have your approval. Let's not fall any farther behind in our quest for customer satisfaction.

The Three Main Parts of Your Presentation

Most presentations can be organized into three main parts: the introduction, the body, and the conclusion. The *introduction* sets the tone for the entire presentation and is your opportunity to grab your audience's attention. A weak introduction can doom the rest of your presentation. If you lose the audience before you even begin, you will have a hard time winning them over again. The introduction constitutes about 10 to 15 percent of your presentation. If you will be speaking for 30 minutes, your introduction should last for approximately 3 minutes.

The *body* of the presentation is organized to deliver your message—to inform or to persuade. In the body of the presentation, use three to five main points, supporting them with data and using transitions to connect your material. You may write out your transitions, but use phrases for the main points. The body constitutes 70 to 80 percent of your presentation. The last 5 to 10 percent is the *conclusion.* This is the last thing the audience will hear and possibly remember. It should neatly tie together everything that came before; be sure to review your main points and give a strong call to action if you want the audience to do something as a result of your presentation.

Use Your Transitions Wisely

To segue from one part of your presentation to another, you will use transitional phrases. These are short remarks that will move you from the introduction to the body of your presentation and from the body to the conclusion. You may also use them to move from point to point within the presentation. Transitional phrases should be written out. They are tools to guide you through and to help you avoid the pitfalls of power robbers or awkward pauses. Helpful transitional phrases are, "Now that we have looked at . . . let's move on to . . . ," or, "We have established the criteria for . . . We can now look at . . ."

Must, Should, Could

Since most presentations run longer than the speaker anticipated, you should be prepared to cut some of your material if needed. An easy way to accomplish this is to color code your presentation into three sections: must know, should know, and could know. Choose a different color marker for each section so you know immediately which section to cut if need be. On your outline, put a box around the "could know" section so you can eliminate it first if necessary. Make sure you remember which color is for which section. If you think you might forget, make yourself a color key at the top of your notes. Then you will only have to glance at the correctly colored section to cut your talk. Don't talk faster to try and get all the information in. It will make your audience nervous, and in your hurry, you may confuse them or leave out important information. With the color-coded method, you will be prepared in advance if you have to cut your presentation.

PUTTING YOUR PRESENTATION TOGETHER

The Introduction

The beginning of your presentation sets the tone for what is to come. It is your chance to make a dynamic first impression, and, as the saying goes, There are no second chances to make a first impression. Your introduction will serve four purposes:

1. Get the audience's attention
2. Establish WIIFT (What's In It For Them)
3. Establish your credibility
4. Let the audience know what your subject is

If you are unable to get your audience's attention right away, your chance to get it later on is practically nonexistent. The best way to focus attention on you is by using a grabber statement or hook to reel in your listener's attention. This grabber can take many different forms. You can tell a story, give an example, ask a hypothetical question, make a controversial statement, use a quote, or use humor. Here are some grabbers that will surely get an audience's attention.

- **Ask a question.**
  If your speech is about unusual vacations, you might start off like this:

  "Have you ever spent your vacation spelunking?" or

> "Have you ever spelunked with a stranger?"

By asking a question, you give your audience something to think about quickly. In this case, what is spelunking or what is spelunking with a stranger all about?

- **State an unusual fact.**

  Sticking with the same subject of unusual vacations, you might start with a statistic, like this:

  > "Only 400 people spent their vacations spelunking last year. I was one of them." or

  > "Last year I got my family to go spelunking on our vacation. We were the only family in Elkins Park to spend their vacation that way."

- **Give an illustration, example, or story.**

  Paint a mental picture for your audience by telling a story that relates to your subject. This will get the attention of and make the content real for the members of the audience. For example:

  > "Last summer I met a man on a bus who convinced me to try spelunking. First he had to tell me what spelunking was." or

  > "Picture this. Two adults, four children, two canoes, four long ropes, a very dark, dark cave, and a guidebook. That was the beginning of our spelunking vacation."

- **Use a quotation.**

  Catchy phrases and quotations can be great openers as long as they have not been overused. Go to the library or search the Internet for unusual quotations or quotations from unusual people.

- **Use humor.**

  If you are going to try humor, be sure that it is in good taste, it is relevant to your speech, you are comfortable using it, and it is funny. When in doubt, try it out on someone you trust. Using humor in front of a large audience is very tricky; you don't know whom you might offend. Humor does not translate well between cultures or even between regions. What's funny in New York City may not be funny at all in Kansas City.

- **WIIFT (What's In It For Them).**

  Don't wait long to get to this point or you will lose your audience's attention very quickly. If your listeners have been told to attend your presentation, or if they are there reluctantly, they will be fidgeting in their seats until they find out whether or not there is some benefit for them. If you haven't convinced them in the first few minutes of your presentation that they will derive some benefit from being there, you will have an almost impossible task ahead of you. Pique their interest quickly. If you notice someone leaving the room, don't let it throw you—people leave presentations for many different reasons. Concentrate on making it the best presentation possible for those who are there to listen to you.

- **Let them know who you are.**

  If everyone in the room already knows who you are, you can skip this step. If not, you need to establish your credentials early on. Let them know why they should be listening to you. Talk about yourself in relation to the topic you will be speaking about. The person who introduced you has probably already listed your credentials, so don't repeat them. But give the audience some reasons to want to listen to you. Although I have been introduced many times, I always try to add something at the beginning of my speech that wasn't part of the introduction. Sometimes I refer to something that has just happened to me or to an experience that sets the tone for my presentation. For example: "I began my training company because I was standing at a bus stop." That statement is a grabber on its own, but it also begins an anecdote that I use to explain how I began my company.

- **Preview your subject.**
  Although your audience probably knows the title of your presentation and may have a general idea of what it is about, it will help them to hear what you are going to be talking about directly from you. If you are giving an informative presentation, tell the audience what you want to accomplish. Be direct and keep it short.

  If your goal is to persuade, you do not have to be quite so specific. You can list several of the points you will be covering and build up to where you want them to go during your presentation.

The Body

Specific organization techniques for the body of your speech will be found in Chapter 4 for informative presentations and in Chapter 5 for persuasive presentations.

The body of your presentation will be answering the audience's question "WIIFM?" ("What's In It For Me?"). The audience will respond to you in one of two ways: emotionally or logically. The body of your presentation will contain elements to satisfy both of these needs. It may contain new material and material that may be familiar but presented in a new way. When you are preparing the body of your presentation, be selective. Not all of the information you have gathered is important enough to be included. You should begin to collect information for your presentation as soon as you have selected your topic. If you will be making presentations frequently during your career, it is worthwhile to keep idea files. Whenever you find a newspaper, magazine, or journal article, or hear something you would like to remember, put it into your idea file. Don't trust your memory. I was once told a story that was so incredible I wanted to use it in a seminar I was leading later that week. I didn't write it down because I was sure I would remember it. The day of the seminar, my mind went blank on the story, and I couldn't tell it to the class. That night I called the person who told me the story, asked her to please repeat it, and wrote it down. It's a story I still tell in my seminars, but it's written down in my files just in case.

When you collect the information that will form the body of your presentation, make sure it is current and accurate. Facts and figures from reputable sources provide evidence to back up your point of view and may help you to sway a skeptical audience to your way of thinking. If your objective is to get the audience to take action, presenting hard data to illustrate what has happened in the past to people who took the same path that you are proposing (or that didn't take it) will reinforce your own viewpoint. For example, I wanted to convince my audience that people who exercise live longer and have a better quality of life. A good approach might be to show hard evidence and statistics to demonstrate that people who exercise regularly live longer and stay healthier longer than people who only eat healthy foods.

You can also clarify your points using examples and stories. If your objective is to have your audience understand that the content of a five-inch can of tuna has decreased over the past several months you could show two equally sized cans and list the tuna content in each. This demonstration allows the audience to see as well as hear your point. The demonstration comes during the body of your presentation.

Using data in the body of your presentation also enables the audience to visualize concepts that do not translate well as visual aids. For example: How many people in your company will be affected if there is a takeover? What jobs will be eliminated? What consequences will those left behind have to face? How will employee benefits be affected? Using data clarifies and makes your points interesting to the audience.

In the body of your presentation, use data in the following ways:

- Examples—add interest
- Stories—let the audience share others' experiences
- Quotations—must be a well-known and reputable source to have value
- Definitions—can help you to prove a point or make a point easier to understand
- Comparisons—present similar features
- Contrasts—present differences
- Statistics—numerical facts and figures to support your points

Using Supporting Materials in the Body

Although you may not be able to convince a hostile audience that raising taxes to build new schools is a worthwhile project for the community, using supporting materials can help you go a long way toward making your point. Begin to collect information as soon as you have selected your topic. Write down everything you know on the subject, what the main points are, and what you need to find out. Be sure that your data are current and accurate. Get as much information as possible to support your position.

Validate your point of view. Although it may be a hard sell to convince the taxpayers of your town that new schools will benefit even those without children, facts and statistics that back up your point of view can help to persuade a skeptical audience of the validity of your arguments. Use facts that parallel your situation. If a nearby community with a similar tax structure has built new schools, and if the community as a whole has had significant benefits, outline them in your speech. Has juvenile crime gone down because the new schools provide better means of recreation for the students? Have property values increased because better schools bring people to a community? These are the kinds of supporting facts that can help you to strengthen your presentation.

Add interest. Raising taxes and building schools is a controversial issue. You can make an unpleasant topic more interesting to your audience by using data to add interest; the number of homes that have increased in value in the area surrounding a new school; the number of jobs created; the decreased rate of juvenile crimes; the added classes available to the community at large in the evenings; and the availability of computers and free Internet access for senior citizens.

Audience involvement. Make your listeners part of your presentation by using the data to involve them. For example, when speaking about building a new school, you could ask them, "How many of you have children who were students at Seaview Elementary school?" or, "How many of you would like to sell your homes, but they're not worth what you paid for them or what you think they should be worth?" After seeing their responses, you could then quote the statistics of what happened to real estate values when a new elementary school was built in the neighboring town and how real estate values go down or stagnate when the schools are perceived as inadequate by potential home buyers.

Look for an emotional connection. If you were to give a presentation on home safety, your points would be remembered if you mentioned Baby Jessica, the little child who fell down a well in her backyard and was finally rescued after several days and hundreds of workers tunneled down and got her out safely. Examples of stories and people who make events memorable can help you to make your own presentation memorable.

The Conclusion

Inexperienced or nervous presenters often miss their final and possibly best opportunity to make their points with their audiences or to ask for a call to action. An effective conclusion should emphasize the key points made earlier in your presentation. If you are giving a sales presentation, this is the time to repeat the product benefits and the benefits to the customer if he or she buys your product. If you are motivating taxpayers to fund a new school, this is your last chance to call them to action and to have them sign your petition. Your conclusion should also provide closure to your presentation and end by giving the audience something to remember. The famous conclusion to John F. Kennedy's inaugural address in 1961 is one of the most quoted historical statements: "Ask not what your country can do for you, ask what you can do for your country." Short, to the point, and memorable. Your closing may not be as memorable as JFK's, but it should have an impact on your audience.

When designing your own conclusion, it is best to present it in two parts: (1) a review of your key points and (2) a memorable final statement or call to action.

1. Reviewing Key Points

- Be brief
- Summarize your purpose
- Answer "WIIFM" for the audience
- Repeat your main points
- Use a transition phrase to lead to your final statement or call to action

2. Final Statement

- Create a new grabber or
- Return to your original grabber or
- Look to the future or
- Call to action

You can create a new grabber for your final statement or use the original from your introduction. For example, if your opening grabber was, "How would you like your property values to go up and the crime in your community to go down?" your closing grabber could be, "If you vote to build a new high school in our community, you will achieve higher property values and lower crime in our community." If you decide to create a new grabber, follow the same rules used for the opening grabber: Ask a question; state an unusual fact; give an illustration, example or story; or present a quotation. If you use your opening grabber, add a new ending or insight. For example, "So, if you want to see your property values go up and the crime in your neighborhood go down, believe the statistics presented here tonight, and vote yes on the new school tax."

Looking to the future reaches out to the audience and gives it a reason to keep thinking about what you have just said. For example, "When the school tax comes up for a vote in November, remember what you have heard here tonight. A new school will raise your property values and lower the neighborhood crime rate. It's a win/win situation for our community."

Suggestions for Effective Conclusions

- The conclusion should be 10 percent or less of your presentation.
- Your style should be consistent with the rest of your presentation.
- Write out the first sentences of your conclusion and outline the rest.
- Test your conclusion by asking yourself these questions:
    1. Does my conclusion help the audience get to where I want it to be?

2. Does it help finish my presentation instead of leaving my audience unsure of what I intended it to know or do?

If the answers to these questions are yes, your conclusion meets the criteria for success.

ADDING EMOTION TO YOUR PRESENTATION

Instead of visualizing yourself as the presenter, imagine you are sitting in the audience. What are your expectations from the speaker? First, you probably don't want to be bored. Then, you might want to be motivated, educated, or convinced, or a combination of these. As in any other situation, your response to the speaker will be influenced by the emotions his or her presentation generates in you. You may not be able to remember the words of the best presentation you have ever heard, but you can probably remember that you were moved by it.

When someone makes a purchase, that decision is usually motivated by emotions. There is usually a rational component to the decision as well, but logic often takes a back seat to emotion. The most effective presenters know how to grab the emotions of their audience and expand upon those feelings to achieve their desired ends. They don't try to knock the audience's socks off or overpower it. They understand where the audience is coming from, and they go forward from there. How will you as a presenter do this?

The first step is to state your goal while you are planning your presentation: "When I finish this presentation, I want my audience to . . . ." What emotions do you want it to have and what actions do you want it to take? If your presentation is about the pitfalls of managed healthcare, here are some of the emotions your listeners could leave your presentation with.

- Concern with their current healthcare provider's service
- Danger of becoming seriously ill
- Worry about out-of-pocket expenses for going outside the system for treatment
- Curiosity about healthcare alternatives
- Desire to find out options available to them
- Motivation to leave the managed healthcare world

Each emotion will lead the listeners to their ultimate action. For different members of the audience, the emphasis will be on different points; their emotions will lead them to what's important to them. Depending on where you ultimately want to lead the audience—for example, if you want them to sign up with your healthcare provider and leave managed care—you will focus on the emotions that are most likely to cause that response. You may want to use a progression of emotions, each leading up to the final decision to leave their providers.

Focusing the Audience's Emotions

As the presenter, you will be directing the audience's emotional focus while you are presenting your material. To do this, you should vary your tone and the speed of your speech. Heighten listeners' attention with changes in your tone to emphasize points: lower your voice to make a very serious point; raise your voice to express disbelief; speak more slowly when making points; speed up to get past less convincing arguments or weaker points. Let the audience experience your emotions with you. If you are excited, angry, worried, afraid—let your emotions come out—the strongest emotions will spread from you to your audience. Have you ever been in a fantastic mood and come into a room full of people? Moods are contagious: others will pick up the prevailing mood in a room and somehow it becomes theirs as well. It is up to you to become a powerful presenter and to let your listeners pick up on your mood. Let your emotions become their emotions and lead them to where you want them to be.

4 Developing the Informative Presentation

Most of the presentations you will give throughout your career will be informative. Your objective is to provide new information or to put a fresh spin on a topic.

Before preparing the presentation, your audience analysis helps you to decide which information is interesting, helpful, or relevant. You do not want to waste the audience's time with material it won't be interested in. If you provide too much information, you risk losing the audience in a sea of confusion. Decide what should be included and eliminate the rest. You can always provide additional facts in a handout or answer questions at the end of your session. If you do not provide enough information, there is also the risk of losing an audience or diminishing your credibility.

There are four essentials to preparing the effective informative speech:

1. **Keep the information fresh.** You are only going to be interesting to your audience if you give it new or updated material. If your topic is already familiar to your listeners, be sure that you have some fact or some new discovery or some exciting theory to share with them. You don't want to see an "I've heard this already" look on their faces or to risk boring them. You won't be asked to speak on this topic again. For example, if your topic is eating a healthy diet to

stay fit, your audience will have probably read or heard quite a lot on the subject. But if your theory focuses on new research you have done or a personal experience that proves your point, it becomes more interesting to the audience.

2. **Make it well organized.** Prepare your information in a manner the audience will be able to understand quickly. If there is a clear progression in the way the information is presented, audience retention will be strengthened. Use key words and repeat them to reinforce your information. If your presentation contains many charts and diagrams, using visual aids that are interactive and that have lots of color may help to keep attention at peak level. Many of the new computer-generated charts make effective use of movement and have information that almost dances around the screen.
3. **Keep it interesting.** Even if you are presenting technical data, try to use colorful language and to project yourself in an appealing manner. This is the time to share interesting anecdotes, bits of historical information, and "what ifs." Use examples, stories, metaphors, case studies, and humor. Bring your audience into the presentation by asking questions or involving listeners in exercises or experiments. Don't find yourself presenting a data dump just to include all the facts. Even the most technical data can be presented in fresh and interesting ways, and even the most interested audience can't track too much information at one time.
4. **Motivate the audience.** Make sure that your information is relevant to your listeners and that you present it up front. A strong start will help you, too, because your listeners will seem more eager to hear what you have to say if they believe that there is something of value in it. Let them know what's in it for them right from the start. If, at the end of your speech, they can expect to increase their productivity or income, tell them. For example, if an audience is made up of prospective buyers of a new product line featuring vitamins and minerals, they need to know that your company is prepared to offer them special incentives.

UNDERSTANDING DIFFERENT LEARNING STYLES

We forget most of what we hear very quickly. Even if your informative speech is full of interesting facts, clever stories, and funny anecdotes, most of your audience will forget the majority of what you have said very soon after it leaves the room. Listeners will probably remember a few key points, and they might even recall the color of your tie or scarf, but much of the information you present, possibly even your name, will not stay with them. (That's why you've prepared good leave-behind handouts!) What can you do to help your audience remember what you said? Keeping in mind that learning styles differ, here are three points to remember:

1. **Repeat yourself.** Tell them, tell them what you told them, and tell it to them again. In the beginning of your presentation, preview your key points. Then use internal summaries to review the points. Be repetitious, not redundant. When giving an informative presentation, it is beneficial, in fact crucial, for an audience to hear the facts more than once. Try to say it differently, review the information, come back to the information, then sum it up. The more times an audience hears your information, the better the chances are that it will remember it. When using visual aids, refer to your chart or other materials when you repeat the data. Don't be afraid of saying the same thing more than once; just say it differently.
2. **Keep it simple.** The things said most succinctly are the things most remembered. Cut your topic into sections and present each one separately. Then review the information to make sure it has been understood. If you are presenting information on your company's new products, don't mention the old products unless they are being phased out or replaced with new ones. Make sure that the information you are presenting is not ambiguous and is targeted to your audience.

3. **Focus on the big picture.** Use concepts instead of details when possible. People are more likely to remember concepts than they are details. If your company is competing with another business of a similar kind, you may have to use details to amplify the differences and to help your company stand out, but use pertinent general principles to make your points. Details can be expanded in your handouts.

PUTTING IT ALL TOGETHER

Once you have chosen your topic, analyzed your audience, and gathered the information, you can begin the final preparations. The informative speech can be organized effectively in one of six ways:

1. **Chronological order.** Arranged in order of occurrence or in a time sequence. If your topic follows a time progression, you might use a time line to illustrate the process. Visual aids can be effective in demonstrating the time span to your audience. See Figure 4.1 as an example.
2. **Spatial order.** Since spatially organized presentations pertain to the nature of space, they are most effective when combined with visual aids. If your presentation is on the effects of classroom set-up on learning styles, you could describe each method, display it as a visual, and explain the way it works. This would help the audience to understand the facts and decide for itself which classroom set-up worked best.
3. **Geographical order.** This presentation is also arranged by space, but by geographical space. If you are discussing the breakup of the Soviet Union, using visuals of how the republics looked in relation to each other both before and after would effectively demonstrate to the audience the different geographical areas involved and their sizes in relation to each other and would help to bring into perspective the vast areas involved.

Figure 4.1

CHRONOLOGICAL ORDER
50 Years of Change in Television Viewing Habits

Date	Event
1947	Black-and-white TVs appear in 5% of U.S. homes. Adults with TVs watch 30 minutes per week.
1957	30% of U.S. homes have TVs. Adults watch 2 hours per week.
1967	75% of U.S. homes have TVs. 50% have color TV. Adults watch 1.5 hours per day.
1977	80% of U.S. homes have TVs. 65% have color. Adults watch 3 hours per day.
1987	90% of U.S. homes have at least 1 color TV. 40% have 2 or more. Adults watch 3–4 hours per day.
1997	95% of U.S. homes have at least 1 color TV. 75% have 2 or more. 85% have cable TV and watch 4 or more hours per day.

Figure 4.2

EXAMPLE OF SPATIAL ORDER
Setting Up Classroom Learning Centers

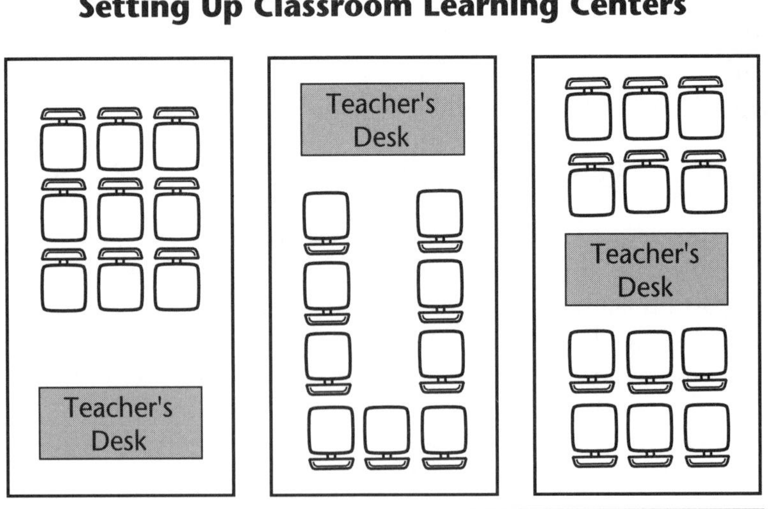

4. **Topical order.** This presentation takes a large topic and divides it. Think of the topic of labor unions in the United States today, and then break it out by union (i.e., teamsters, garment workers, auto workers, etc.) and by which unions had members in which states.
5. **Comparison and contrast.** This presentation compares characteristics, features, and qualities that are similar and then contrasts their differences. It helps to clarify the unknown by comparing it to the known. If you are trying to explain a topic such as global warming, for example, compare it to something that everyone can relate to, such as warming a house. Use examples of how the process of global warming operates by relating them back to how home heating works.
6. **Cause and effect.** The presentation organized by cause and effect has a distinct order. First comes what has happened, or what will happen, and then comes what the results will be. For example, if your company stops subsidizing medical benefits for some employees but not all employees, the end result will be a lot of unhappy employees and some resentment. You can also give multiple scenarios and conclusions using the cause-and-effect format.

After determining your method of organization, it's time to put it together with the rest of the information you have gathered. The Informative Presentation Planning Sheet (see Figure 4.3) is a tool that can help you with the process.

Skill Drill

Develop a five-minute informative presentation on why you chose your college major. Videotape and record yourself. Watch, listen, and critique your performance.

Figure 4.3

INFORMATIVE PRESENTATION PLANNING SHEET

The purpose of the speech is to: ______

Method of organization: ______

Audience description: ______

Introduction

Grabber: ______

WIIFT (What's In It For Them): ______

Source credibility: ______

Preview statement: ______

Body

Supporting material and transitions should be included in this section.

Main point: ______

Supporting details: ______

Transition: ______

Main point: ______

Supporting details: ______

Transition: ______

Conclusion

Review: ______

Memorable statement: ______

Ten Commandments of Informative Presentations

1. Less is more.

What should be your measure of success when it comes to an informative presentation? Answer: How much the audience comprehends and retains, not how much information you gave out. Don't do data dumps.

2. It's a jungle to the audience.

You've been through this material; your listeners often have not. You've been there; they haven't. Walk them through the material and give them plenty of landmarks so they can maintain their bearings. Provide multiple internal summaries. Review. You're the tour guide; don't charge through this jungle of information and lose your audience along the way.

3. Assume they don't understand.

When in doubt, assume that your audience will benefit from the extra effort you take to make something understandable. An extra example or analogy or a rephrased explanation helps more often than it hurts.

An audience is more likely to get frustrated by a lack of understanding than impatient with your extra efforts. When feedback satisfies you that the majority have grasped what's being said, move on.

4. Keep relating back to what they already know.

You provide your audience members with hand-holds when you relate new material back to things they already know. Highlight similarities and point out notable differences. Memory is based on association; help them by linking new information with knowledge they already have.

5. Use visuals and simplify.

If people see as well as hear the concept you are explaining, they comprehend it faster and retain it better. It is important that your visuals are simple, clear, and representational.

6. Keep lingo and jargon to a minimum.

All industries have their own language, their lingo or jargon. This language may be second nature to you as a presenter but may not be to your audience. For the sake of those who may not understand your jargon, either explain it as you go along or leave it out.

7. Insist on interaction.

Whenever possible, avoid straight lecture. Constant feedback from the audience is particularly important if you are presenting complicated, technical, or unusual information. You need to test the level of understanding regularly in order to know if you are succeeding with your presentation. Encourage questions. Ask questions. Don't fear audience interaction; it helps you know what level of understanding is being achieved and enables you to make adjustments to your presentation if necessary.

8. Demonstrate.

When possible, go beyond visual to actual demonstrations of the concepts you are covering. The impact on the audience can be dramatic, increasing comprehension and memorability.

9. Do the unexpected.

Most audiences walk into a presentation with a certain amount of cynicism. While protocol may dictate a certain presentation format, little warning bells should go off in your head when you hear yourself saying, "This is how we always do it." Is it really proper protocol, or is it a rut you and your fellow presenters are in? You want to capture your audience's attention and generate interest in what you have to say. Try something new, different, unexpected. Technical presenters, don't let the fact that the material is on the dry side be an excuse for not trying to make it interesting.

10. Sell!

You're not part of a sales force but you still have to sell. Your listeners are going to make an effort to pay attention if they perceive a benefit to themselves. You cannot afford to assume that the value of what you are saying is self-evident. Point out the value. Point out the benefits. Point out the possibilities. If your audience members don't want this information, they're not going to try to absorb it. You have to answer their WIIFM (What's In It For Me).

5 Persuasive Presentations

Have you ever ordered anything while watching a TV commercial or infomercial? If you answered yes, you have responded to a persuasive presentation. If you have ever purchased an automobile, you have experienced still another form of persuasive presentation. These are two very extreme forms of persuasive presentation yet, in and of themselves, very successful ones. The Saturn line of cars are sold with still another form of persuasive presentation—the reverse sales method. Saturn commercials focus on the fact that Saturn cars are different. Their dealers won't haggle over price, and they won't just sell you a car, they'll make the experience pleasant—you'll enjoy it so much that you may buy more than one or even spend your vacation visiting a Saturn manufacturing facility.

How can you be persuasive? By using various methods of proof. Aristotle talked about using *logos, pathos,* and *ethos,* and they are just as valid today.

Logos in Greek means reason, and is where the word *logic* is derived from. It contains your facts and figures, statistics, and other forms of documentation. This type of information can be slanted to support the presenter's own philosophy. Just listen to any politician at election time.

Pathos, also from the Greek, refers to using emotions. This is the method for appealing to the needs, wants, and desires of your audience. Most decisions are made using a combination of logic and emotion (*logos* and *pathos*). Understanding the needs of your listeners is vital to persuading them. You want them to feel good about their decisions, and you can combine *logos* and *pathos* to accomplish this. While many scientific thinkers claim to use only logic to make decisions, the human part of us is more subtly influenced by emotion than we may care to admit.

The third mode of proof is *ethos,* or credibility. How are you perceived by your audience? What are your credentials, and are you a credible speaker on the topic? Many people vote strictly along party lines regardless of who is the candidate. Their parties' candidates are perceived as being the best for the job strictly because of party affiliation. Credibility is not at issue for the individual candidate, only for his or her party. If the party loses face, the candidates will suffer as well. Since decisions were made strictly by *ethos,* the candidate's individuality didn't matter.

ESTABLISHING CREDIBILITY

What are the major components of credibility? Credibility consists of three components: *perceived trustworthiness, perceived competence,* and *perceived conviction.* Regardless of whether or not the presenter actually has any of these things, the audience's perception is what matters. If the audience perceives the presenter as trustworthy, competent, and having the power of his or her convictions, that is what is important. It is then up to the speaker to confirm what the audience believes.

If, however, credibility is an issue, how do you deal with it? Your competency can be established by your introduction, which states your credentials and accomplishments. The force of your convictions will be established during your presentation as you demonstrate your knowledge and display your convictions. Your trustworthiness, however, is more difficult to establish. A classic approach to establishing trust is through common ground. It involves sharing the similarities between you and your audience—common demographics, attitudes, and experiences all count toward establishing trust. For example: "I've lived in Chicago for the past 30 years, as have many of you. I am a product of the Chicago public schools, as are many of you. I've been paying Chicago city taxes for the past 15 years, as have many of you. And I want to pay less—as do many of you." You have established common ground—where you live, where you went to school, the fact that you pay taxes, and your dissatisfaction with the taxes you pay. All these common bonds count toward establishing trust with your audience.

Most successful presentations have some elements of all three modes of persuasion. The speaker's style and analysis of the audience and topic help him or her decide how much of each to use. In addition to having three possible modes of persuasion, persuasive presentations also have three levels of persuasion: *to motivate, to convince,* and *to call to action.*

The first level of persuasion is *to motivate.* You want to excite your listeners about what is being shared with them, but you probably won't be altering their opinions or beliefs. Motivation can be as familiar as a church sermon or a speech by the coach of a sports team getting his players fired up before their game. You want your listeners to feel good about what you are telling them and about themselves.

The second level of persuasion is *to convince.* You want your listeners to change their opinions or to develop the same opinion you have. You may not want them to do anything but change their minds. If they haven't yet formed an opinion, you want them on your side. If your office is currently using Mac computers and you are positive that PCs will offer much more, you want to convince the office manager or other person responsible that PCs are the way to go.

Then you move on to the third level of persuasion, which is *a call to action.* You want the audience to do something, perhaps vote for your candidate, donate money to a specific charity, hire you, or, in the case of the office manager, purchase PCs for the office. This is the most difficult level of persuasion to achieve.

Any persuasive presentation can be prepared using the same method. Developing an outline will be the first step. Following the format provided here, first state your purpose: motivate, convince, or call to action. You may want to do a combination of two—for instance, convince and call to action. Be clear about your objectives. You will ultimately use your purpose to determine the effectiveness of the presentation.

Next, identify your audience and the attitudes you will be facing: *favorable, hostile, apathetic, uninformed,* or a combination (*favorable mix* or *hostile mix*). In order for your presentation to be effective, you need to have an understanding of who you will be speaking to and, you hope, something about their mindset. When determining audience attitude, keep the following in mind.

Favorable audience. They already share your opinions and probably want what you want. The office manager may have a PC at home and think it's great but perhaps hasn't thought about using PCs in the office.

Hostile audience. Understand why the audience is hostile: is it your topic, request, or philosophy, or is it just a hard group to win over? I was once hired to give a presentation on training techniques and when I entered the training room and went to introduce myself, no one greeted me. I wanted to diffuse the situation right away, so instead of opening the session by talking about my listeners' objectives for the sessions, I asked them to discuss their objections. Now they knew I would be listening to them, and they began to open up and talk about their problems and why they felt hostile. One of the things they objected to was the program's starting time; we had started at 7 and their day started at 6:30, so I said we'd start at 6:30 the next day. This made them feel that I was listening to them and dealing with their objection.

On another occasion, I was asked to facilitate a program that was being rolled out to a sales department who thought it was a waste of time. Their feelings were obviously negative, so I opened by asking them about why they were against the program. After listening to why they didn't think they needed the training, I was able to turn things around by telling them about improvements that came from the program. I was also able to ask them about areas where they could improve their skills, and I listed some ways they could accomplish this. They soon began to see that I was interested in helping them improve the skills they felt they wanted to work on. I demonstrated that I understood their concerns and was there to work with them.

Apathetic audience. Your listeners really don't care about what you have to say and must be made to realize how they will benefit before they will respond favorably. For example, senior citizens in your community may not care if a new playground is built because they no longer have young children, even if the funds are already in place and it won't cost them anything. You will have to use examples of how they will benefit from the playground (it may be used by their grandchildren or other family members or for senior–kid events, etc.) to convince them that the playground is a worthwhile project for them to support.

Uninformed audience. Your listeners are not opposed to what you have to say; they just don't know anything about it. This audience takes more time to develop but your goal is clear. Your job is to educate them. For example, if you want me to give money to neuter cats and dogs in the neighborhood and I'm not a pet owner or a pet lover, you will have to demonstrate to me that there is a need and how our neighborhood is being affected by an overrun of stray animals.

Mixed audience. There are two types of mixed audiences: the favorable mix and the hostile mix. The *favorable mix* includes favorable, uninformed, and apathetic members. You will have to inform the uninformed and convince the apathetic that there is a real need or benefit. If there is even one hostile member of the audience, the crowd can shift and align itself with the hostile member. If this occurs, the group is identified as a *hostile mix*. Your audience analysis should have prepared you for the hostile mix, and your challenge is to disarm the hostile members and win them over as soon as possible. Sometimes the real audience isn't even in the room—members have brought the opinion of someone else with them. If you are prepared for a hostile audience, you will be ready for any mixed group.

The hostile mix is probably the most difficult audience to work with. Organize your presentation to bring up comments like, "If we go with this procedure, what are the benefits to your department?" If the hostile mix audience believes that you are receptive to its concerns and not afraid to talk about them, it will be more apt to listen to your points later on. It is up to you to determine and address the reasons for hostility. It probably has nothing to do with you personally. There may be budget cuts, unfair promotions, or other grievances that have nothing to do with what you want to talk about. A good listener will gain the respect of the audience. If you are presenting information that you know will be received negatively, bury the negatives in the middle of your presentation and end with the positives. Don't be evasive; you will be found out sooner or later.

After determining your purpose and audience, think about the logistics of your presentation. How long will you have to present? What time of day will you present? Are you part of a group? How large is the audience? Where will you fit in? Next, collect your information. Make sure this information is pertinent, current, accurate, relevant, and appropriate. For example, if you will be speaking about cuts in funding for education in your community, make sure you have the facts and can support them with evidence. If you are appealing to your audience for funds and sense hostility because taxes are high or perhaps their children are already out of school, you will have to find their "hot buttons" and appeal to them on that level. Perhaps you have research that proves that community spending to improve the quality of education leads to lower crime rates and increased property values—you will be able to relate the information, meet the audience's needs, and keep your own agenda at the same time. Prepare your data keeping the audience and its attitudes in mind at all times.

Finally, decide on how to organize your presentation. There are four options available: *proposition to proof, problem to solution, reflective,* and *motivated sequence.*

1. Proposition to Proof. In this method, your proposition is stated at the beginning of a presentation. This lets your listeners know right up front what you want from them. Then you prove your proposition with three to five points of evidence and an emotional appeal. Finally, you review the evidence and end with a strong closing statement. Since you want your listeners to be receptive to what you are going to say, you don't want to offend them in the beginning of your presentation or they will be closed to your point of view. To make people want to change their points of view, give them new information presented in a way that they will be able to understand easily. This method works well with favorable audiences and is possible with some work for uninformed, apathetic, and favorable mixed groups, but it is not a good choice for hostile or hostile-mix audiences. See Figure 5.1.

Figure 5.1

SPEECH PLANNING WORKSHEET

Type: Persuasive
Organizational Style: Proposition to Proof

Central Theme: Consider: Purpose, Audience, and Logistics (PAL™)

Proposition:

Proof:

Introduction	
Grabber:	**Source Credibility (optional):**
WIFFT (optional):	**Preview (optional):**

Conclusion
Review:
Memorable Statement / Call to Action:

Example of a proposition to proof situation

Proposition: You state your proposition—"I recommend that the company change to PCs and use a Windows-based operating system." This is why:

- More business software is available.
- We will get better service.
- Our clients are using PCs. We can work more easily with them.

2. Problem to Solution. In the problem to solution method, you state the problem and then present a solution from your point of view. The audience must believe that there is a problem and agree that it must be solved. This must be done before getting to the solution. No solution will solve a problem we don't have. If the problem is complex, make sure you spend enough time detailing what the problem is. After you have explained the problem clearly, offer your solution being sure to include three to five points and supporting material, a review, and a memorable closing statement. This works for the same types of audiences as proposition to proof. See Figure 5.2.

Example of a problem to solution situation

Problem: Our company cannot get the software it needs to develop important sales reports because the software is not available in Mac format and our company uses Mac computers. This is causing lost time for the sales people, who must do needless paperwork. I also believe that this problem is costing our company a great deal of money.

Your solution: By switching from Mac equipment to PCs, your company will be able to purchase the software the sales force needs to free them from the hours spent doing manual reports. Although there would be an initial adjustment period while they learned the new system, the training time is usu-

Figure 5.2

SPEECH PLANNING WORKSHEET

Type: Persuasive

Organizational Style: Problem to Solution

Central Theme:
Consider: Purpose, Audience, and Logistics (PAL™)

Problem Definition:

Proposed Solution:

Introduction	
Grabber:	**Source Credibility (optional):**
WIFFT (optional):	**Preview (optional):**

Conclusion
Review:
Memorable Statement / Call to Action:

ally only two days. The cost for the new PCs could be easily recouped by the increase of sales (projected at 35 percent) when the sales force is able to spend more time selling and less time on paperwork. This new system would enable them to spend more time in the field with customers as well as more time developing sales leads. This in turn will result in increased sales and a more content sales force. I have attached a cost analysis to today's agenda detailing how the new systems would work. If we switch to PCs before the end of this quarter, we have the potential to gain more than $400,000 in additional sales at a cost to us of only $50,000.

3. Reflective. With this method, start with a problem and then prove that it exists. This begins the same way as problem to solution. Prove that the problem exists, then establish the criteria to evaluate and select a solution. Explain the solutions that you are rejecting, including the benefits of these solutions, then negate them by proving that the only possible solution is the one you are espousing. See Figure 5.3. The risk of this reflective method is that the audience may not be sure of what you are advocating. If you are not strong in presenting your beliefs, you will not be able to convince others that your way is the best. Leave no loopholes; make sure that you have eliminated other points of view as viable, leaving your solution as the best choice. This is an excellent approach for analytical people who love to evaluate all details. It can be overkill for favorable, uninformed, and apathetic audiences if they are not detail-oriented. This approach can work well with hostile and hostile-mixed groups.

Example of the reflective method:

Problem: Each member of the sales force (10 people) spends approximately 10 hours per week generating manual sales reports. During these 100 cumulative hours per week, no sales are made and no leads are generated. If the sales force had

Figure 5.3

SPEECH PLANNING WORKSHEET

Type: Persuasive
Organizational Style: Reflective

Central Theme: Consider: Purpose, Audience, and Logistics (PAL™)

Problem Definition:

Criteria for Judging Possible Solutions:

Possible Solution:	**Possible Solution:**	**Possible Solution:**
Positives: Negatives:	Positives: Negatives:	Positives: Negatives:

Introduction	
Grabber:	**Source Credibility (optional):**
WIFFT (optional):	**Preview (optional):**

Conclusion
Review:
Memorable Statement / Call to Action:

access to Windows NT, it could use software that would cut this time down to 2 hours weekly, leaving 8 additional hours per person to generate income for the company.

Optional Solutions:

#1: Hire a new person to do the manual sales reports for all of the sales force. This would free up the sales force but would mean the additional expense of another person, who would not be generating any income at all and would cost salary plus benefits. The sales force would still have to spend time relaying the information to this person. **#2:** Get new Mac software which isn't as good as the Windows NT but would probably free up the sales force by about 25 percent. New software would be expensive and would probably be obsolete within a short period of time. It still wouldn't provide the sales force with significant additional time, but it is better than the current situation. **#3:** Do away with all manual paperwork, get the sales force new PCs with Windows NT. Sell the existing Mac computers or trade them in for the new equipment. This will help to defray some of the cost of the new equipment and the additional income generated by the sales force would pay for the new equipment within three months. The sales force would be happier and more productive and the benefits to the company would far exceed the cost.

3. Motivated Sequence. This is the method used the most in sales. It leads your audience to a call to action. A presenter leads the audience to the brink of action and then provides it with the means to act. With the other methods, you have to build in a call to action yourself if you want to include it. The motivated sequence either creates a need in the audience or makes it aware of a need. You then supply the means to satisfy that need. It is up to you to make the solution appealing to your audience. See Figure 5.4.

Figure 5.4

SPEECH PLANNING WORKSHEET

Type: Persuasive
Organizational Style: Motivated Sequence

Central Theme: Consider: Purpose, Audience, and Logistics (PAL™)

Need (problem):

Satisfaction (features):	**Visualization (benefits):**

Introduction	
Attention (grabber):	**Source Credibility (optional):**
WIFFT (optional):	**Preview (optional):**

Conclusion
Review:
Memorable Statement / Call to Action:

Example of Motivated Sequence:
Attention: Are you holding yourself back in your career because of your inability to present your ideas?
Need: In order to become an effective sales person, you must be an effective presenter. Studies show . . .
Satisfaction: If you take a Brody Communications Ltd. seminar you will learn how to:

- organize your ideas
- read your audience
- control your stage fright
- move and use visual aids
- handle questions comfortably

Visualization: With these skills, you will be able to connect with your audience and sell your ideas. Picture yourself as a regional sales manager . . .
Appeal to action: Call Brody Communications Ltd. at 1-800-726-7936. The time to start is now.

Knowing how to present persuasively is critical to career development and will benefit you in other areas of your life as well. The ability to influence other's beliefs and motivate change is a powerful tool to be used carefully and selectively.

Skill Drill

Develop a five-minute persuasive presentation choosing one method of persuasion. Videotape and audiotape yourself. If you are unsure whether or not you have been persuasive, ask someone to listen to your speech. Choose another method and develop another five-minute speech. Videotape and audiotape yourself again. Critique your performance and make adjustments as needed.

Four Models of Persuasive Speaking

1. Proposition to proof:

- Grabber statement
- State your proposition
- Proof—Using logic and emotional appeals
- Review
- Memorable statement—Ask for what you want. Draw conclusions.

2. Problem to solution:

- Grabber
- Problem—Be sure to prove that a problem exists. This could be a big part of the presentation. No solution is necessary if the audience doesn't recognize the problem.
- Solution
- Review
- Memorable statement—Ask for what you want. Draw conclusions.

3. Reflective:

- Grabber
- Problem—Establish criteria to evaluate and make a decision.
- Possible solution
- Possible solution
- Possible solution—End with your choice.
- Evaluate all solutions using the criteria, making sure that the solution you are advocating best solves the problem.

- Review
- Memorable statement—Ask for what you want. Draw conclusions.

4. Motivated sequence:

- Attention
- Need—Create plan.
- Satisfaction—Talk about how your plan satisfies the need.
- Visualization—Paint a positive picture of the benefits of your plan.
- Appeal to action—Get a commitment if possible.

PERSUASIVE PRESENTATIONS AT TRADE SHOWS

The audiences you will encounter at a trade show are very different from others. Instead of delivering a presentation to an invited audience, you are in competition with trade booths, technological wizardry, freebies, food displays, and a myriad of other distractions for your potential audience. But people have stopped at your booth, and now it is up to you to make it work. They will probably not give you too much time unless you get them interested right away. In Chapter 14, you will learn some audience involvement techniques which will further help you to develop your trade show persuasive presentation.

There are four basic elements used in the creation of an effective trade show strategy: creativity, simplicity, consistency, and interactivity.

1. **Creativity.** Make them stop at your booth. They may stop because you have a product or a service they might need.

But your competition around the corner is giving out freebies and that is not in your marketing plan. You need a hook to capture the audience's attention. This should be a unique idea that brings your message to life. Surprise them, startle them; you need to get their attention now. You want your presentation to create drama and impact.

2. **Remember the acronym KISS?** Keep It Simple Speaker. Too much information will lose them. Be clear and concise. Research indicates that the average trade show attendee spends about seven hours walking around the show. You won't have any time to waste. People who are asked to sit at your presentation for very long will become resentful and will flee from your booth the moment your presentation is over. And it's doubtful that they'll be back.
3. **Be consistent.** Since most people have an attention span of only 90 seconds, and at least half of what is heard is forgotten in under 60 seconds, now is the time to tell them what you want to tell them, tell them again, and then tell them again what you just told them. Be consistent and clear. Benefits-oriented messages will work best when you don't have much time to be persuasive.
4. **Interactivity will help your listeners to remember your message.** Since you won't have much time to make your points, help them to remember by giving them tools—now is when an interactive device or a game may help your product or service to be the one people are lined up outside the booth to see. Keep things pertinent and relevant to your company, and try to make it fun.

Trade Show Tips

- Talk to the crowd before you present. This helps to break the ice and gives the presenter some information about whom he or she will be presenting to.
- Work as a team. Select a leader and have each member assume an active role in the presentation. One might be a coordinator who signs up potential customers or clients for the presentation and follows up

by getting business cards or lead generation forms. One might be the person who handles questions and answers. Another can be in charge of passing out materials as well as of meeting and greeting.

- Don't forget the "WIIFT" (What's In It For Them) when creating your presentation. If they don't find the benefit to choosing your booth over a competitor's, your booth will empty out fast.
- Practice, practice, practice. A well-prepared and practiced effort will help your booth and its presenters to stand out from the competition.
- What is your purpose in speaking?
- How does your audience feel toward you and your purpose?
- What emotional and psychological appeals will move them?
- What logical facts will influence them?
- Are they open to new ideas?
- What's in it for them?

Entertaining/ Special Occasion Presentations

Speaking at a special occasion is unlike making an informative or persuasive presentation. The goal of these speeches is to be inspirational, so choosing the right words and coming across to your audience as sincere are important. Vivid language will help you express your thoughts about the occasion. Your words should arouse emotion and focus the audience's thoughts and feelings on who or what is being honored or commemorated. If you read your speech, you will not seem sincere, it is therefore essential that you know your key points and introduction cold.

Your technique and organization skills are not as important because there are clear expectations of what your speech should contain. For example, if you are paying tribute to someone who is retiring after 25 years with the company, the audience will expect to hear glowing praise, a funny anecdote or two about the person, and maybe that person's future plans. If you were presenting at a roast, you would expect to be telling stories at the honoree's expense. All in fun and good taste, of course.

Many speakers believe that every speech should start with a joke. Jokes can grab an audience's attention, but unless you are a professional speaker or comedian, and positive that your humor will be appreciated—and that it is really funny—you should not tell jokes when asked to speak at a special occasion. That does not mean you won't be able to use humor; it simply means that jokes are best left to professionals.

When you are asked to speak at a special occasion, it will probably be to introduce other speakers; to speak at testimonials, banquets, or ceremonials; or to deliver welcome or exit speeches, perhaps even a eulogy. It is important for you to understand what is expected of you and for you to perform accordingly.

THE WELCOME PRESENTATION

The welcome presentation is designed to welcome people into companies or organizations or groups to events and is generally a short speech used to begin an event or occasion. This type of presentation sets the mood and flow of upcoming events and outlines the occasion for the audience so it knows what to expect. The expectation is that the speaker will associate the values of the welcoming group with those values possessed by the person being welcomed.

Example:
Good morning associates, family, and friends. The board of directors and I would like to welcome you to our first annual employees and family day. Today will give all of you, and all of us, the opportunity to learn about each other and our families as we join in games and activities designed to further the goals of our company.

Welcome speeches are also used to begin occasions such as wedding receptions, awards banquets, and dinner receptions, and they tend to have a strong impact on the audience. They give the event organizers, hosts, or sponsors an opportunity to show who they are and what the event is about and will set the tone. The welcome speech is an opportunity for you to distinguish yourself. If you do a good job welcoming your boss to his anniversary dinner, you may find yourself asked to give a more prestigious presentation.

SPEECHES OF INTRODUCTION

A strong introduction should generate enthusiasm and give the listeners a quick overview of the person they are about to encounter. It should include accurate information and enhance the impression of the person about to make his or her way to the platform. A good introduction generates excitement and enthusiasm for the upcoming speaker or performer and makes the audience receptive to what is going to be said or done.

Example:
Marjorie Brody has a secret. This secret has led her from the quiet life of a college professor to the platform of some of the world's most prestigious organizations. Marjorie Brody knows the secret of using personal marketing to make life-changing events happen. Today, she is going to share that secret with you, and then days from now you will be able to change your life as well.

An introduction can ruin the entire event if it detracts something from the person being presented or his or her presentation. Be careful not to give misleading, useless, speculative, or untrue information. Finally, be sure that you pronounce the person's name correctly. When in doubt, ask him or her before you go out in front of the audience. If you are being introduced, it is a good idea to write your own introduction and send it in advance to the person doing the introduction. Bring an extra copy to the event.

ACCEPTANCE SPEECHES

You've just won the Employee of the Year award at your company, and during the luncheon in your honor you will be making an acceptance speech. This isn't the Academy Awards, and it's also not the time to be dramatic. Be sincere and let your thanks be heartfelt. Thank the person or persons giving you the award and anyone who inspired or helped you, including your family. A gracious and sincere acceptance speech will be remembered, and you will be seen in a positive light. Acceptance speeches are common in the world of business, politics, and entertainment.

Example:
I feel like I have grown up at Brody Communications. And it's been a wonderful experience for me. Today, you are honoring me by naming me "Employee of the Year"—but I would like to honor you. Having the opportunity to be a part of a company like Brody Communications has taught me about the important things in a career—the opportunity to grow, to experience loyalty, to develop my skills, and to be appreciated for them. To my co-workers and to those who granted me this honor today, I say thank you.

INAUGURATION SPEECH

An inauguration speech is usually given by a person who is assuming the head position of an organization or government. Such speeches can include those delivered by the incoming president of a club or the president of an association. The objectives in this type of presentation are to reaffirm the values of the organization you are about to head and to state the goals you will attempt to achieve while in the head position.

Some goals to keep in mind:
Note the accomplishments of your predecessor, highlight your own accomplishments without bragging, include the direction you and your team would like to take, and make everyone there want to be on your team.

EULOGIES

If you are asked to say a few words about someone you have worked with (or for), keep your remarks short and tactful. Although you and Jim might have had some great times after work at the corner pub, this is not the time to mention them. Be respectful of the family and remember that your boss may be there listening to you (and judging you).

Example:
Jim and I spent the past 15 years working side by side at Plaza Computers. He was a thoughtful co-worker and good friend. I will miss sharing ideas with him and learning from him . . .

THE TOASTMASTER

The toastmaster is the person who conducts the event. It can be a company dinner, retirement party, roast, birthday, or even an event for visiting delegations of some kind (students, politicians, foreign visitors, etc.). It is the responsibility of the toastmaster to play a leading part in running the show. He or she makes sure everything goes smoothly and on schedule and plays a part as master of ceremonies or moderator. The toastmaster gives the opening remarks, leads the group into the meal, introduces other speakers, and closes the event. If awards are to be handed out, the toastmaster may perform that role as well or introduce those who will be doing it. If there is to be a question-and-answer period, it is also the job of the toastmaster to facilitate this. The toastmaster should communicate in advance with other speakers to make certain procedures are clear and to assign time slots. If things drag, the toastmaster should tactfully step in or alert the speaker that time is running out. It is also up to the toastmaster to avoid putting anyone on the spot who does not wish to speak. This is especially true during ceremonies at which those honored are surprised and may not wish to speak.

NEW EMPLOYEE ORIENTATIONS

These events are often coordinated by the Human Resources departments in large companies. As part of an orientation program, you may be asked to speak to a group of new employees or trainees. Get specific information as to what is expected of you, who else will be speaking and the topics they will be covering, and the amount of time you have for your presentation. You will be giving the new employees information about your area of expertise and your presentation should take into account the limited amount of knowledge they may have about how things work at your company. This is an occasion to provide information and to generate a positive impression of yourself and your department. As you will probably be presenting as part of a group, respect the time constraints. If there will not be enough time to answer questions, offer new employees the best method or time to contact you for additional information. If you will be representing your department, check with others you work with to see if they would like you to include any information you may not have thought of.

THE FAREWELL SPEECH

These speeches are commonplace today as people change jobs, and careers frequently. If you will be speaking on your own leaving, mention some of the memorable experiences you shared with the people there and indicate how these experiences have contributed to your growth and enjoyment. It's a time you can single out people who made a significant contribution to your work experience and say thank you to them. If you are speaking about someone else who is leaving, pay tribute to them by recognizing their contributions to the company.

USING STORIES & ANECDOTES

When a businessperson is asked to speak at a special occasion, you are not the entertainment. But you can use humor naturally by telling your own stories and anecdotes. It is a good idea for you to compile a collection of your own humorous stories or stories you have heard that you will feel comfortable sharing with the audience. An advantage of telling your own stories is that they help to build rapport with the audience. This is true with co-workers and employees who will see you in a new light as you share a part of yourself with them. If the stories are work-related and you all work in the same company or industry, there will be a unique feeling of relating, you to the audience and it to you, as you share in your story. Your own stories need not be strictly work-related. You can use humorous anecdotes from your own life, for example:

- trips you have taken
- your family
- your childhood
- your own career path
- your hobbies

- your friends
- your own embarrassing moments
- your fears

By sharing your own personal stories, you will quickly make a connection with the audience, and it will be more receptive to whatever comes next in your presentation. A word of caution: If you are delivering a special occasion speech that is negative—because, for instance, it addresses company downsizing or a reduction in stock price—this is not the time to begin with a humorous anecdote.

Some Guidelines to Consider Before Using Humor

- If humor does not come naturally to you, don't use it until you are comfortable using it. Practice at least three to six times and if it still doesn't come out comfortably, leave humor out of your presentation.
- If you are not comfortable with long stories, use one-liners.
- If you're not sure something is funny, try it out on a friend, spouse, or co-worker. If in doubt, leave it out.
- Try to surprise your audience with your humor; don't start off by saying, "I want to share this funny story with you." Better to surprise them with it.
- If no one laughs, try to say something to ease the silence, for example: "That's the last time I ask my attorney if something is funny."
- Don't laugh too hard at your own jokes—it's OK to let your enthusiasm for the anecdote show, but laughing too hard is in poor taste.

If You Choose to Use Humor

You can use humor successfully if you stick to the guidelines. First, make sure it's appropriate for the occasion. Unless it specifically pertains to your company, you're sure everyone there will understand it, and no one will be offended, proceed with caution. Inside company jokes can be very funny, but only if everyone gets the joke. When used properly, humor can be a wonderful icebreaker. In a room where few know each other, it can make friends out of strangers and sympathetic listeners out of apathetic ones. Stories about yourself are safest; everyone enjoys a good joke at someone else's expense—when it's done with tasteful good humor and the joke is told by you about you. If you have decided to use humor, here are six guidelines to help you:

1. **Remember the punch line.** A great story isn't so great if you can't remember the end. You will also lose credibility with the audience.
2. **Make sure that the anecdote relates to your speech and is appropriate.** Don't speak about your children's exploits when the group includes infertile couples.
3. **Have good timing.** Practice your anecdote. Tell it to several people and watch their reactions. If the story doesn't go over well, modify or eliminate it. Practice until you feel comfortable with the material.
4. **Don't be cruel.** You might think fat jokes are funny, but it's likely that someone in the audience has had a weight problem or is sympathetic to someone who does.
5. **Don't use vulgar language.** Even if your audience is a room full of "the guys," it's never appropriate.
6. **Humor doesn't travel and it doesn't work overseas.** This is true even regionally within the United States. Always keep your audience in mind; what's funny in New York may not be funny in Memphis.

Remembering humorous anecdotes may seem easy when you first hear them or think of them, but chances are, just like anything else, you'll forget the whole story at a later time when you want to use it. Save yourself some grief and write the story down as soon as you think of it or hear it. Then when it's time to prepare your presentation, you'll have a collection of humorous anecdotes ready to use.

Skill Drill

Prepare a five-minute presentation welcoming prospective clients to your organization. Use stories and anecdotes pointing out some of the potential benefits of doing business with your company.

7 Team Presentations

Many of the opportunities you will have to present throughout your career will involve other speakers. These occasions may take the form of panel discussions, symposia, forums, new business presentations, contract renewals or awards, meetings, and other group situations. To be effective, team presentations must be meticulously planned and executed. They must be like a ballet, in which each dancer knows exactly where to stand, when to move, and when to exit from the stage. Stakes are often high, as, for instance, when advertising agency teams, often with the same levels of experience and creativity, compete for advertising contracts worth millions of dollars. What makes one team stand out? Presentation dynamics. If a team works like a smooth, well-oiled machine, if one member's presentation flows into the next presentation, and if all members present themselves professionally and intelligently, the impression left is one of confidence and competence. Team presentations come with their own unique set of problems. Decisions have to be made in concert with the other team members, and this can lead to confusion and controversy. It is therefore essential to have one strong team leader who will guide and coordinate all members' presentations, making sure that each person has his or her area covered adequately and that one member's presentation does not duplicate someone else's.

Six Steps to a Successful Team Presentation

1. **Pick the right leader.** Often the person with seniority is automatically designated team leader. This may not work if that person is busy with other projects or has too much day-to-day responsibility to spend the time necessary coordinating all members' presentations. The team leader should be the person who has most knowledge of the topic or the client, who is respected by the other members, and who is known to be objective and therefore able to give them fair criticism.
2. **Agree on the focus.** Each member of the team should be aware that his or her contribution is essential to the success of the presentation and that no one member's part is more important than another's.
3. **Schedule frequent updates and reviews of the material.** Each member of the team should be discussing his or her part of the presentation with the team leader to ensure that he or she is headed in the right direction. Group meetings should be held so everyone is aware of where the other members are heading.
4. **Conduct proper audience analysis.** Team presentations are usually given to other teams. This means that the listeners may come from different levels in the organization, from different departments, and have different agendas of their own. Each member of the presenting team should understand who the listeners are and their knowledge levels and interests should be considered.
5. **Pay attention to details.** The leader or a designate should have responsibility for the details such as room arrangements, equipment, visual aids, and

handouts. Everything in a team presentation should be coordinated and reviewed well in advance of presentation day. This person should also arrange for the team to practice in the room where it will be presenting if possible.

6. **Have mutual respect for team members.** The group dynamics will be apparent to the audience. A team in which the members work well together, respect each other's part in the presentation, and enjoy being together will have the advantage. If your team is made up of people from different departments who may not have had the chance to meet, schedule an informal lunch or dinner so they can have the chance to get to know each other. The comfort level the members have with each other will help them to relax and do their best during the presentation.

IF YOU ARE THE TEAM LEADER

If you are the team leader, much of the planning and details will be your responsibility. The other members of the team will be looking to you for guidance and for validation that their presentation will be effective. To ensure the best outcome for your team, your responsibilities should include the following:

- **Buy-in of the concepts and strategies from management.** It is up to you to schedule a meeting with key people *before* the team begins working. This will avoid the team having to do things over again later if management doesn't agree with the direction you have taken. The support of management will be important to team members and will help to encourage them.
- **Audience analysis.** As team leader, you should gather information about the audience. If another member of

the team has more contact with the audience, assign that person the job of preparing the audience analysis. It should include key players and decision makers.

- **Define the strategy for your team.** You have met with management and mapped out a strategy for the presentation. It is up to you to meet with your team and to make sure that each member is comfortable with the strategy. It is also up to you to give a clear picture of the audience and marketing strategy to those members of the team who may lack insight into these areas.
- **Assign the topics.** If you have chosen your team or had them assigned to you, as leader you will most likely be assigning each presenter his or her topic. In creative presentations, writers and art directors know what their areas are, but it is still up to the leader to explain what each member of the team is expected to do.
- **Make a schedule.** You should schedule time for individual meetings with each presenter and for the group to meet for run-throughs and updates. This will give each team member the chance to familiarize him- or herself with the others' work and to see how the presentation fits together.
- **Provide strong leadership and direction.** The team members will be looking to you to make sure everything is on track. It is up to you to stay on schedule, on budget, and on course. Failing to provide strong leadership may result in missed deadlines, extensive rework, and an unhappy team. This will lead to poor performance.

IF YOU ARE THE MODERATOR OF A PANEL DISCUSSION

- It is your responsibility to introduce the topic to be discussed and to introduce each speaker. It should have been decided beforehand whether the moderator will give the panelists' credentials or whether each panelist will give a brief introduction of his or her own.
- You will be opening and closing each segment of the discussion. It will also be your responsibility to maintain

proper timing, giving each panelist a fair time share. The moderator keeps track of how long each speaker has to make his or her point and gives each speaker a warning when time is running out. If the speaker keeps going over allotted time, it is up to the moderator to stop him or her.

- The moderator will also provide a bridge between segments and may or may not comment between presenters. He or she may simply move the discussion along if comments are not appropriate.
- The moderator opens the question-and-answer session, paraphrases the questions, and calls on the person who will respond. At the end of the question-and-answer period, it is the moderator's responsibility to end the discussion and sum up.

SUCCESSFUL MEETINGS

Many of the presentations you will give throughout your business career will be at meetings. On average, executives spend more than 50 percent of their time at meetings. Whether that time is well spent is the question. If you are asked to arrange a meeting, your first task is to define the purpose of the meeting and to determine if a meeting is the best way to address the issues. What is the purpose?

- To solve a problem
- To share information
- To plan a strategy
- To gather information
- To provide instruction
- To showcase someone's abilities
- To brainstorm ideas
- To review data

When a meeting is planned without thought given to its purpose, the attendees often arrive with competing or conflicting perceptions of why they are there. An agenda or memo defining the purpose of the meeting should be distributed to all invitees prior to scheduling the meeting. This way, if there is another way to accomplish the purpose or an alternative method of dealing with it, you will find out in advance.

If a meeting is needed, who should attend? The purpose of the meeting should determine who needs to be there. In large corporations, representatives from various divisions may be needed; in a small organization, just a decision maker and one or two others may be sufficient. In selecting whom to invite to the meeting, your objectives as a presenter should be considered. If you are not the organizer but have been asked to present, there may be someone in the organization whom you want to hear your presentation, either because it affects him or her directly or because you want them to see you in action. Request that this person be invited and let the organizer know why.

Successful meetings require careful planning. If you will be creating the agenda, how should you present the information? Agendas should be brief and to the point. You could use phrasing in the form of questions, each accompanied by a brief statement of justification for including the item on the agenda. If the agenda is covering only one topic and various participants will be presenting segments, use the purpose as the title of the meeting and include each participant's segment, name, department, and title. It is important to include a timetable. A sample agenda appears in Figure 7.1.

A properly planned agenda helps the meeting to flow smoothly. Presenters know in advance how much time they will have, and the leader is able to keep things on track. The leader of the meeting will not necessarily be the senior person there. However, if you are the leader and your superior is there, you must decide where to include him or her and make it clear to the other participants who will be taking a leadership role during the meeting. Otherwise you may find

Figure 7.1

SAMPLE AGENDA

January 24, 1998 10:00 A.M.–12:00 NOON

"Recommendations to Replace Office Computers"

10:00	Opening remarks	M. Remey, Office Manager
10:10	Overview of current system	M. Brody, VP, Operations
10:30	Feasibility of updating current equipment	L. Alfaro, Systems Analyst
11:00	Options for replacing system	A. Abrams, Systems Analyst
11:30	Cost variables for both options	A. Frieman, Controller
11:45	Summation/recommendations	M. Brody

yourself losing control when others look to the highest-ranking person for input.

During the meeting, the leader should take just a few moments between each participant's part to summarize the meeting's progress (e.g.,"We now know what updating our current computer system will involve, so let's begin to explore our other options."). At the final segment of the meeting, the leader should take the time to check with the participants for consensus (e.g., "Do we all agree that we need to make changes in our computer system?") Allow each person's thoughts to be heard and, within the time constraints, to be discussed. If there is a lot of disagreement or dissension, the leader may wish to discourage discussion and to schedule individual meetings to avoid further conflict.

Obstacles to Effective Meetings

Two of the more common obstacles to effective meetings are the floor hogs and the reluctant speakers. To make a floor hog ineffective, do the following:

- Interrupt him midflow with a question that can be addressed to someone else.
- Don't call on him—avoid eye contact.
- Speak with him or her privately during a break or ask a superior or someone in authority to speak with him or her.

With a reluctant speaker,

- ask him or her a question you know he or she can answer.
- praise his or her contribution.
- go around the table for comments, forcing him or her to participate.

The effective meeting leader persists in making sure that terms are clearly defined and assumptions clarified. In times of conflict, the leader must refocus the meeting back to its purpose and end the conflict. The leader must know when to stop an unproductive meeting.

ENDING THE MEETING

Every meeting needs closure. It is the responsibility of the leader to summarize the key points made by all presenters (you should be taking notes throughout the meeting to enable you to do this) and to give the next steps or call to action:

- Restate the purpose of the meeting.
- Summarize the key points.
- Delegate follow-up assignments.
- Announce the next meeting.

8 Using Visual Aids Effectively

Our ability to retain information increases by close to 40 percent when visual aids are used. That means that you, as a presenter, have a greater opportunity to make an impact on your audience when you use visual aids—properly. By using visual aids, you help the audience to see what is being discussed. Their use allows complicated information to be broken down into parts, making audience comprehension easier. The speaker also benefits. Visual aids allow you to move and to have something to do. They can also remind you of what to say and when to say it. They can help to reduce tension and stimulate interest.

There are four basic rules to follow when using a visual aid:

1. **Leave it up long enough for your audience to look it over before you begin talking about it.** Keep it simple enough so that the audience isn't reading while you are talking.
2. **Don't talk to the screen, talk to the audience.** Stand so that the visual aid is to your left. Point with your left hand (which will be at the beginning of the sentence).
3. **Practice before your presentation** so that you are comfortable working with the visual aids and equipment.
4. **Keep going if something goes wrong with the visual aids or equipment.** Turn the machine off if necessary and proceed without any visual aids. Remem-

ber: The visuals are an aid for the audience, not you, so be prepared to present without them.

TYPES OF VISUAL AIDS

The days of simple flipcharts aren't quite over—they are still useful for small group meetings and presentations, but today's technology has created new classes of visual aids to add to the more traditional modes. To determine which method works best for you, practice using a few different types before you make a final decision. You may wish to use more than one type of visual aid during your presentation, for example, flipcharts and overheads or slides and video. You may find that the type of visual aid you choose depends upon several variables:

- the length of your presentation
- the audience size
- the logistics of the meeting room
- the available equipment
- the type of presentation you will be giving

Don't get so comfortable using one type of visual aid that you are reluctant to try anything else. Even the same presentation you have given 50 times will take on new life with a new type of visual aid. When you practice your presentation, visualize yourself presenting with overheads, then with slides, or even with a complete multimedia show. Use your imagination and your visualization skills, and then try something new.

Flipcharts

A flipchart is a large pad of paper mounted on an easel. It is bound at the top and loose at the bottom. As you fill up one page (using magic marker), flip it over and start another.

(There are now electronic flipcharts. A camera can capture the image, and it then gets printed.) Flipcharts are best used in small, informal groups.

You can write as you speak, or you can put your points on the flipchart in advance of the meeting. You can add points as your meeting progresses. A flipchart can look sloppy by the end of your presentation, and it can be hard to go back to a previous point.

When writing on a flipchart, use large letters, and use blue or black marker only. Never use red and green together as many people suffer color blindness with these colors and will not be able to differentiate your points. Leave room between your points—follow the four-by-four rule: use no more than four lines and four words per line on any flipchart page. Write only on the top three-fourths of the page. Some presenters write their points in pencil, very lightly, in advance of presentations. Then, during the presentation, they are able to write their points in marker. If you have written very faintly, the audience may not even notice the penciled notes. This is also good for diagrams and graphs.

When presenting from flipcharts, be sure to stand on the correct side. If you are right-handed, the flipchart should be to your left during the presentation. When you begin to write, move slightly to the left and you will be in the correct position. For left-handed presenters, do the reverse.

Remember the three Ts—touch, turn, and talk—as you use your visual aids. You are speaking to the audience, not to the flipchart. After you touch your key point, turn to the audience, establish eye contact with someone, and continue to talk. Use the hand closest to the flipchart when touching it.

If you are presenting in a room with soft walls, use push pins to attach the finished pages to the walls so the audience can see what has already been discussed. You will also be able to add things if needed.

Tips for Flips

- Use flipcharts only during small-group presentations.
- Leave it covered until you are ready to use it.
- Black or dark blue markers are best—use a color such as red only for emphasis.
- Never use more than four lines of four words each.
- Write large enough so those in the back of the room can see.
- Pre-write your notes or charts lightly with pencil.
- Stand on the correct side of the flipchart when presenting.
- Remember the 3 Ts—touch, turn, talk.

Graphs and Charts

Simply constructed graphs and charts help an audience to grasp your point, make comparisons, or view specific items in relation to the whole.

Graphs

- Line graphs make it easy to illustrate trends and show increases or decreases in a quick way (see Figure 8.1a).
- Profile graphs use shading underneath the data and make it easy to see large or significant changes (see Figure 8.1b).
- Bar graphs let your audience see blocks of information, allowing them to make visual comparisons quickly (see Figure 8.1c).
- Pictographs use figures rather than a line or a bar to show the same type of information (see Figure 8.1d).

Figure 8.1

GRAPHS

a. Line Graph

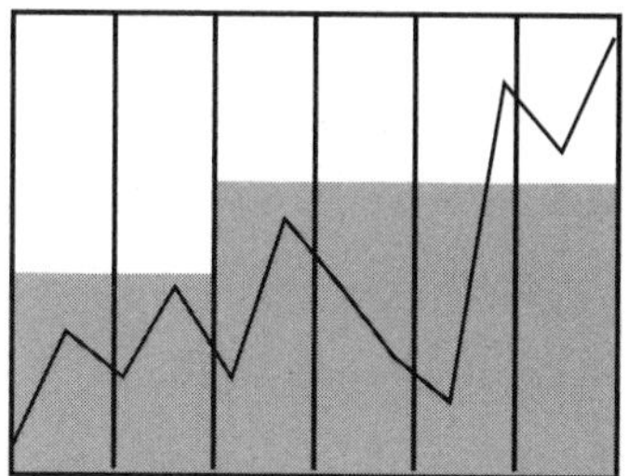

b. Profile Graph

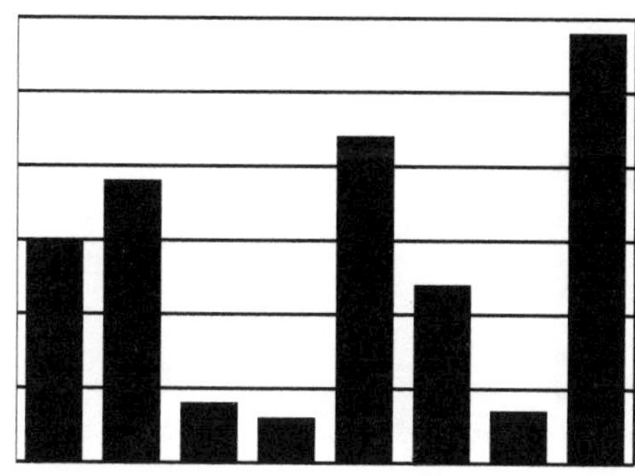

c. Bar Graph

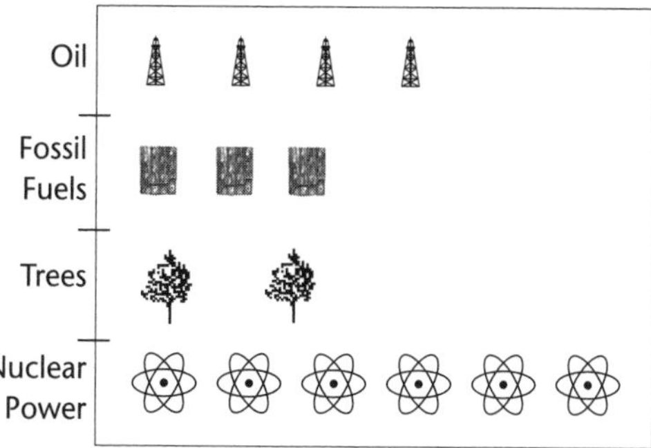

d. Pictograph

Figure 8.2

CHARTS

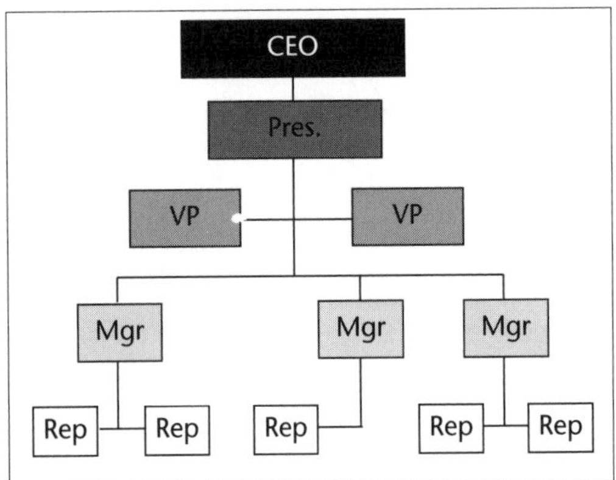

a. Organization Chart

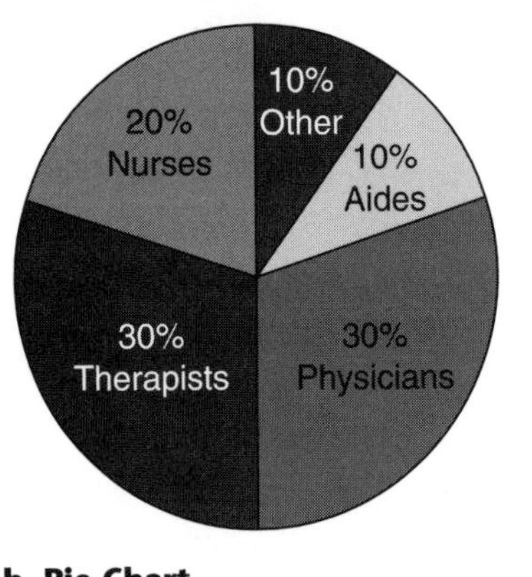

b. Pie Chart

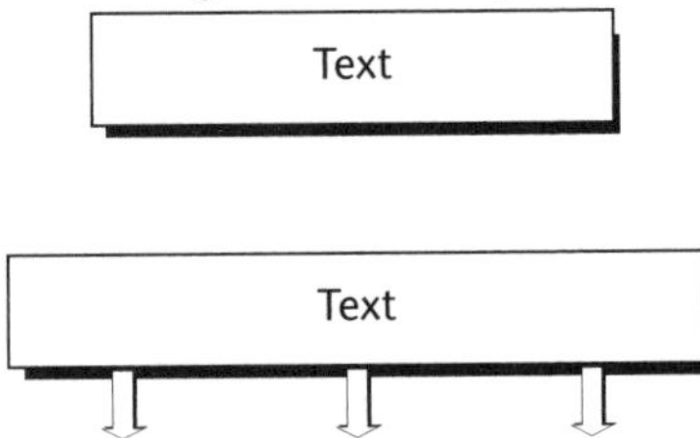

c. Flow Chart

Charts

- Organization charts help to clarify complex subjects or procedures (see Figure 8.2a). They are useful for detailing social groups or chains of command. They can help your audience to see and understand your subject quickly.
- Pie charts clearly depict pieces in relation to the whole and to one another (see Figure 8.2b). It is a way to simplify a combination of details for your audience.
- Flow charts show a series of sequences or relationships in an easy-to-follow format (see Figure 8.2c).

Overhead Projection

Even though we live in a high-tech world, the overhead projector is still the most commonly used method for displaying visual aids. Nearly every conference room or meeting site has one, and many presenters have their own. There are small, portable ones that are easy to transport and not very expensive. Unfortunately, many presenters use poor quality overheads, which detract from, not enhance their presentations.

Overhead projection requires the following equipment: an overhead projector (with a working bulb), clear plastic sheets called transparencies, markers or grease pencils, and a method of concealment. The transparencies are placed one at a time on the glass surface of the projector. They are illuminated by the bulb and a lens projects the image onto a screen or blank wall. Professional-looking transparencies must be made well in advance of your presentation. You can make them yourself using a computer and printer. The images will be large enough to be seen by a large group or small enough for conference-room meetings.

Overheads are often used to excess. Many people put their whole presentations on transparencies, forcing the audience to read and watch the screen instead of the speaker. They should be used to enhance the key points of your presentation, not serve as a substitute for it. You don't want the audience reading when it should be listening.

When you create your transparencies, use color for emphasis. The typeface should be no smaller than 18-point in an easy-to-read font. Use no more than four lines and four words on any given line. Maintain proper margins and stay in the top three-quarters of the page.

Purchase frames made to hold the transparencies. The frames keep the transparencies from sticking together and also protect the transparencies, which can be stored in a binder. Number your transparencies and place them in order before your presentation. Mark the order on your speech outline. There is also a product on the market called Instaframe. This is put onto a projector and the transparency is placed into it. You adjust the frame's position until the transparency is correctly placed on the screen. As you present, each transparency will be perfectly positioned by keeping the Instaframe in place and putting each subsequent transparency into it.

Touch, Turn, Talk

When presenting, do not stand at the overhead projector. Stand to the side of the screen and use your left hand or a pointer. Touch, turn, and talk to the audience. If you are not using the pointer, put it away. Don't use it for any other purpose than pointing at the screen—don't use it to point at your audience.

Remember that there are many different types of overhead projectors. Make sure you arrive early enough to turn on the machine and make any needed adjustments. Check the neck to make sure it projects high enough onto the screen so your audience can see the transparencies. Carry an extension cord in case you want to move the machine and an extra light bulb in case one burns out. Make sure you know how to replace the bulb in advance. When you are not using the machine during your presentation, turn it off and move away so your audience is not distracted.

Slides

Slides have lost favor with many presenters but are still widely used, especially for scientific presentations. They can be easily made on your computer and work well for large group presentations.

The best slides have dark backgrounds and light typeface. This allows you to keep a few or all of the lights on during your presentation. When you turn all of the lights out, people get sleepy. Limit the number of slides you use and keep the wording brief. Pie charts and simple graphs work well. Using several colors will help to differentiate your points.

When presenting, stand at the front of the room and face your audience. Use a remote control to change the slides. If you have trouble differentiating between the forward and reverse buttons, put a piece of tape on one of them so you will be able to distinguish them by touch. Before your presentation, make sure you have checked that all of your slides are in correct order and position. An upside-down slide or one that is from another presentation will make you look unprepared. Carry an extension cord and extra bulb just in case. When you finish with the visual aid, turn the projector off and raise the lights if they were dimmed.

Video Systems

Video systems can be used for a variety of purposes: playback of prerecorded tapes; computer-controlled presentations using video monitors or projectors; live video of remote events; recording and playing during a presentation. Because video systems usually involve several pieces of equipment, planning, prechecking, and rechecking are essential.

Keep in mind that if you are not bringing your own equipment with you, video playback systems vary. The VHS format tape is not compatible with either the Beta format or the 8mm format. Make sure you have checked the compatibility before using any tapes. An on-site inspection of the equipment and the room where you will be using it will save you embarrassing problems later on.

If you will be recording as well as using playback, make sure you have made your requirements known when requesting the equipment. When I videotape the participants at my seminars, conferences, and workshops, I usually bring my own equipment, including two camcorders and my own tripod. I bring two cameras in case one breaks down. Since playback equipment is too heavy and cumbersome to transport myself, I arrange for it to be on-site when I arrive. I always arrive early enough to arrange the proper lighting and test all the equipment so I won't have to spend time making adjustments when the audience is in the room. If I am going to be audiotaping, I make certain I have extra extension cords, batteries, and tapes, and I test the equipment myself before I begin to tape during the presentation.

Video Monitors

What size monitor should you use to make sure everyone in the auditorium can see properly? Here are some general guidelines:

Audience size	Monitor size
10 or under	19 inches
11–25	25 inches
26–75	4–6 feet

For larger audiences, several large monitors will be needed.

LCD Panels and Projectors

Liquid Crystal Display (LCD) panels are fast replacing slide presentations. They are connected to the video port of a computer and let you project images on a blank wall or a screen. Combined with a laptop computer, they are easy to use and fairly simple to transport. LCD panels and projectors enable you to use higher-quality graphics and visuals in your presentation.

LCD panels are designed for use with overhead projectors (for good quality images, the overhead projector should produce a standard measure of light of no less than 4,000 lumens). The LCD panels themselves are flat devices that are about the thickness of a laptop computer and weigh about seven pounds. The screens range in size from 8 to 10 inches and can project images as large as 10 feet. The panels can change screens quickly and produce clearer images and better color reproduction than can other methods of projection.

The LCD projectors are self-contained units combining LCD display, a light source, and projection. Although they are heavier than LCD panels, you have everything you need in one place. There is no need for an overhead projector. Since the light source is built in, it can be matched to features of the LCD display, producing higher-quality images. This technology is changing rapidly. The weight and cost are decreasing and the resolution is getting better.

Multimedia Presentations

Multimedia presentations are no longer the domain exclusively of professionals; you can create your own using a computer. There is software available that will allow your computer to display digital video sequences, to transport your audience to out-of-sequence slides, and even to incorporate other presentations. Multimedia presentation computer packages may include drawing tools for graphics creation and prescripted buttons that can be set to trigger internal events such as starting a video sequence. Most entry-level multimedia presentation packages can produce transition effects (wipes, dissolves, etc.) and moving-typeface-style animations that let you sequentially march topics onto the screen. You will also be able to incorporate movies into your slides using programs for either Mac or Windows. In addition, some programs have begun to incorporate hypertext-like features that can impart interactivity to your presentation, like, for example, on-screen buttons to transport the audience to out-of-sequence slides or even to other presentations.

Depending on the needs of your audience, you can alter the content of your presentation on the fly. There are also entry-level programs that enable you to integrate text, graphics, audio, animation, and video elements into well-coordinated presentations. In addition, most multimedia presentation programs come with prescripted buttons that can be set to trigger internal events, such as starting a video sequence, or used to launch other linked presentations. Because these programs are constantly changing, it's best to read up before purchasing one.

Computer Presentation Reminders

- Check your set-up and power sources. Bring a pair of screwdrivers along with your computer in case you need to connect cables or peripherals.
- Bring extension cords, power-surge protectors, and cables you might need.
- Bring duct tape and scissors to secure wires to the floor and walls so no one will trip.

- Be sure your power pack is fully charged or new batteries have been installed.
- Carry an auxiliary light with you or request one if the room will be darkened.
- If you are using a modem, verify that the room has compatible phone jacks and that they work.
- Have duplicate copies of your software with you.
- Run through your presentation using the computer visuals and make sure they can be seen from all seats.
- Practice using the equipment until you are completely comfortable with it.

WRITING FOR VISUAL AIDS

When preparing your visual aids, remember that their purpose is to enhance your presentation, not detract from it. What you are going to say is the most important part, and good visuals will help you capture and hold your audience's attention. When writing your visuals, remember the following points:

Typeface

Choose one that is easy to read. Sans serif type is ideal for headlines, serif is better for text (sans serif lacks "feet"). Be consistent and use the same font for all titles and the same for all text. Don't use more than two fonts.

Keep It Simple

Reading too many words will tire your audience. Use words to describe your points and summarize when possible. Save the complicated information for your presentation and handout.

Be Consistent

On a single visual, if your bullet points are in the form of questions, keep them all questions. If they are in the form of statements, keep them that way.

Titles

Limit the title of a visual to one line and subtitles to two lines. Don't put the title of the program on every visual or they will begin to look cluttered.

Capitalization

Do not capitalize all words in bulleted text. IT'S TOO DIFFICULT TO READ. Use initial capitals for titles. Capitalize only the first word and any proper names.

IN SUMMARY

Visual aids need to be planned, executed, and used wisely. The effective presenter has spent time to develop visual aids, is familiar with them, has practiced using the aids, and handles them easily and smoothly. Your audience and topic will help you determine which type of visual aid to use. The location of your presentation may dictate the method you choose. Always make sure you have verified the available equipment and power supply before deciding which type of visual aid to use. If possible, have a backup system with you just in case. Be prepared to give your presentation without visual aids; after all, things go wrong with even the best-prepared events.

Visual Aids Reminders

- Check the room set-up and equipment availability before preparing your visual aids.
- If possible, practice using the visuals on-site.
- Arrive early on the day of your presentation to have adequate time to set up equipment.
- Carry extra bulbs, extension cords, duct tape, scissors, and tools.
- If using computers, make sure all electrical outlets are grounded.
- Make sure your power pack is fully charged or new batteries have been installed on your laptop or hand-held computer.
- Make sure proper phone jacks are available if you are using a modem.
- Make sure the keyboard operator has an auxiliary light if the room is to be darkened.
- Bring duplicate copies of software.
- If renting or borrowing equipment, make sure you are familiar with it in advance of your presentation.
- Make sure your visuals can be seen from every seat.
- When using slides, make sure they are in order and none are upside down.
- Make sure everything is spelled correctly, especially customers' names and products.
- Be prepared to speak without visuals just in case!

HANDOUTS

Handouts are typed pages pertaining to your presentation and contain materials you want the audience to have. They can have copies of charts, slides, or graphs or other visual aids as well. They can be an outline of your key points or contain information you have chosen not to include in your presentation. They should be neat and well-presented and have your name, address, telephone and fax numbers, e-mail, and web address on them (if you would like your audience to be able to contact you). They can also contain biographical information about you and may give some background facts about your company or service. Their purpose is to enhance your speech, not to detract from it, so make sure they are clear and easy to read.

Handouts are a good idea to use if

- your speech contains a lot of technical information
- you can't put all the information in your speech
- you want your audience to take notes during your speech (make sure to tell them when it will be appropriate to take notes)

You don't want your listeners to take notes during your speech. Make sure to tell them that the information is available in the handout, so they won't need to take notes.

Always tell your listeners what is in the handout and when they should use them. If you don't want them to read the handouts during your presentation, don't give them out until the end.

Skill Drill

Add visual aids such as flipcharts or overheads to the five-minute informative presentation you previously prepared. Videotape your presentation, self-critique, make corrections, and tape again.

Room Arrangements

How the room is arranged for your presentation should be to your benefit as a presenter. Many times, however, there will be fixed seating or you will be unable to make an advance request for the arrangements you prefer. You may find yourself speaking in a room that has another purpose the rest of the time, or you may be in a state-of-the-art conference center.

Either way, it is up to you as the presenter to be prepared. You should telephone ahead to find out as many details about the room arrangements as possible. If you have any special requests, this is the time to ask. Will you need a microphone, any special extension cords, an overhead projector? Ask. Also find out how the room will be set up, if the seating is fixed, the size and number of tables, or if it is to be auditorium-style seating. Your goal is to arrange the seating to suit both you as the presenter and your audience.

PREPARING THE ROOM

If you are on-site, prepare the room by sitting in different parts of the room to make sure you can be seen from every chair. Move furniture around if you have to. If you will be using visual aids, set them up and test again from seats in different parts of the room. It is more annoying to the audience if they can't see your visuals clearly than if you use none at all.

If you will be presenting to a large audience, have the room set up in a classroom or theater (see Figure 9.1a) or crescent shape (see Figure 9.1b). These arrangements have the audience in front of you and your visual aids beside or behind you. This type of seating works best for large groups and presentations that do not involve participation.

If you will be presenting to a group of 25 or fewer, and you anticipate interaction, a U- or V-shaped arrangement is preferable (see Figure 9.1c). You are in the open area and your visuals are in the center. This set-up works best for small groups and for presentations that include participation. It does not work as well for large groups because the shape becomes too wide for you to see those sitting in the corners.

If you will be speaking to a very small group, conference style works well, with the group sitting in either a circle, square, or at a conference table. This will enable the participants to interact but will make it difficult for you to address those directly on either side unless you step well back from the table.

PRACTICE ON-SITE

If possible, it is advisable to practice your presentation in the room where you will be giving it. This will enable you to check your equipment and get comfortable in the room.

Make sure the podium or lectern is placed where you want it. If someone will be speaking before you, note where you want it placed in case it is moved prior to your presentation.

Standing behind the lectern for any length of time is not a good idea. It separates you from your listeners when your objective is to bring yourself closer to them; speakers who spend their entire presentation behind the podium are perceived as aloof. Step out from behind the podium and move closer to the audience. If you are nervous and need to refer to your notes, walk behind it again when you feel the need. Speakers of short stature sometimes cling to the lectern

Figure 9.1

SEATING ARRANGEMENTS

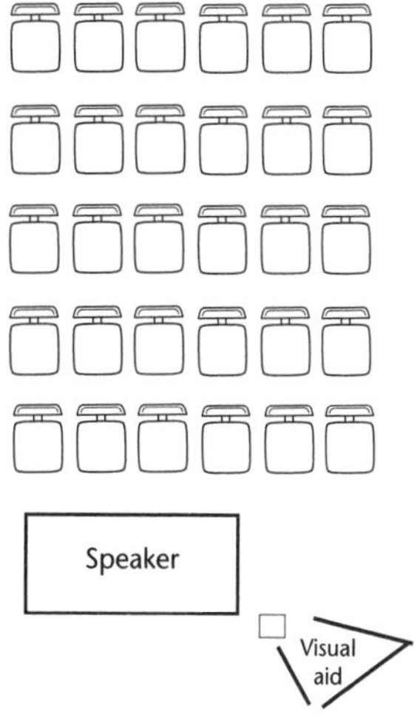

a. Classroom- or Theatre-Style Seating

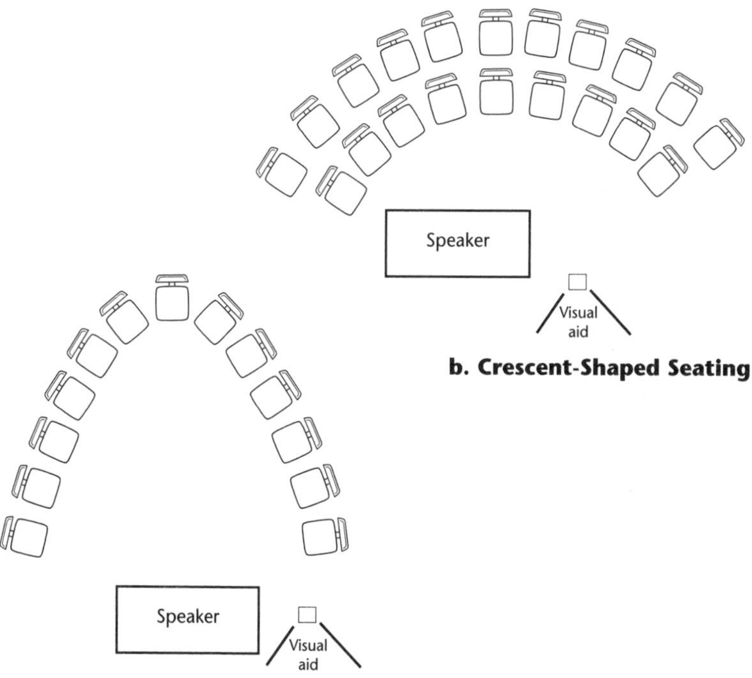

b. Crescent-Shaped Seating

c. U-Shaped Seating

because of the riser placed behind it to make them tall enough to be seen above it. A better choice is to walk forward and stand closer to the listeners. It will help to establish good rapport with them.

If you are forced to stand behind the podium because that is where the microphone is located, consider requesting the use of a cordless microphone, or buy your own. If you haven't used a wireless mike before, familiarize yourself with it well in advance of your presentation so you are not fumbling with it and can turn it off and on with ease. Remember to turn it off as you leave the platform so that any private remarks you may make are not overheard by the audience. I always tell my classes the classic story of the speaker who took a break from her presentation. She was so comfortable with her wireless microphone that she forgot about it and so forgot to turn it off when she went to the restroom. She was still there when a woman burst into the restroom yelling, "Your mike is still on!" Needless to say, she never forgot again.

There are several different kinds of microphone on the market today. Get comfortable with as many models as you can as you may not know what is available where you are presenting. Or bring your own along.

- **Lavaliere.** Hangs around your neck, allowing you freedom of movement. You need to be careful of the cord.
- **Clip-on.** Attaches to your clothing. Many lavalieres are also clip-ons.
- **Table microphone.** Rests in a holder that stands upright on a table. Allows you to move in front of or behind the table.
- **Floor microphone.** Rests in an adjustable, free-standing holder. Can be placed anywhere in the room.

NOT TOO HOT, NOT TOO COLD

Unlike Goldilocks, you will not have the chance to sample different rooms before you find the one that is just right, so it is up to you to make sure that the environment is comfortable and conducive to learning. Check the air conditioning, heating, and ventilation system before your listeners arrive. If it is too warm, they will become sleepy and have trouble concentrating. If it is too cold, they may be uncomfortable. However, if a lot of people will be in the room, lower the temperature to 65 degrees to compensate for the rise in temperature caused by body heat. Better a bit cold than too warm. Also make sure that the room is well ventilated by a door, window, or fan.

NO DISTRACTIONS, PLEASE

If you will be speaking in front of a window or in a very bright room, pull the shades down to eliminate glare. Sunlight in the audience's eyes will make it difficult for people to see you or your visual aids. If the room has moveable chairs, position the listeners' chairs so that their backs are to the door so there is less distraction if participants enter or exit the room.

Room Arrangement Checklist

- The room is set up to your specifications and is of adequate size for the number of people expected.
- A microphone is available or you have your own.
- Practice your presentation where you will give it.
- You can be seen and heard from every seat.
- All electrical outlets and extension cords are where needed.
- You have backups: bulbs, extension cord, visual aids, etc.
- The ventilation system is adequate.
- The room temperature is 65 degrees.
- The window shades are down to eliminate glare.
- Participants' chair backs are to the door.

10 The Five Styles of Delivery

Different speaking situations call for different styles of delivery. These styles are identified as *impromptu, extemporaneous, expromptu, manuscript,* and *memorized.*

1. IMPROMPTU STYLE

Also known as off-the-cuff speeches, impromptu speeches are given on the spur of the moment. You were not previously informed that you would be speaking at an occasion such as a meeting, but you may be asked to give a status report on a project, to comment on a proposal, or just to give your opinion about the topic under discussion.

Most presentations are impromptu, and you can be prepared to present even when you haven't been able to prepare in advance. The secret to being successful at impromptu speaking is to relax and let your knowledge of the subject work for you. If you are going to a meeting, come prepared and expect to be called upon for your input and opinions. That way it won't come as a surprise when you are asked. When you know your subject well, it is easier to relax and speak.

If you are going to a meeting and suspect that you may be asked for an opinion, do some homework on the topic being discussed so you will be able to add your input to the occasion. For example: You are going to a meeting at which the topic is whether your company should change from the HMO it has a contract with to the traditional fee-for-service plan it formally used. Although you have not been specifically asked to speak, you are fairly certain that your opinion will be solicited because you have been with the company since its fee-for-service days. You have opinions, so now is the time to jot down your thoughts and to be prepared. If you are asked to speak, you are ready. If someone else speaks first and says the same things you were thinking, you will at least be able to agree and explain why.

Many businesspeople use impromptu speaking as a way to test their knowledge and the knowledge of colleagues. Successful impromptu speaking offers you an opportunity to shine and thereby to impress colleagues and perhaps your boss. In group situations, impromptu speaking can become brainstorming that results in new ideas.

2. EXTEMPORANEOUS STYLE

In the delivery style most frequently used by speakers, extemporaneous presentations are planned, prepared, and practiced. They are polished presentations that may be given many times but should never be exactly the same. You may use an outline or notes, but the speech should never be written out or memorized.

An extemporaneous speech may sound spontaneous, but it isn't. Each and every detail has been planned in advance, including anecdotes and illustrations used to make your points. Because what you want to say is planned, you are able to change things around to adapt to each individual audience each time you give the presentation.

Politicians frequently give extemporaneous speeches. For example, during his 1996 presidential reelection campaign, Bill Clinton spoke extemporaneously about welfare reform in every city he visited. Each time, however, his message sounded slightly different. He was able to adapt his message to his audience and to the region of the country where he was speaking.

3. EXPROMPTU STYLE

A combination of extemporaneous and impromptu styles of delivery, the exprompt u speech is prepared but not practiced. Occasions when you could be asked to give an exprompt u presentation include meetings, conferences, and debates. When you are asked to participate, have some time to put your thoughts together, but don't really practice. Your success as an exprompt u speaker depends on how well you gather and organize thoughts. On these occasions, you still have time to write an opening sentence that will set you up to make your points. Use notes to help you organize your thoughts. Write a closing sentence to end your presentation; this will also serve to let your audience know you have finished speaking.

4. MANUSCRIPT STYLE

A manuscript speech is written down and read word-for-word to the audience. It is widely used in the scientific community, in which technical papers requiring exact wording are submitted for presentation, accepted, and then read by the author. Politicians, teachers, and trainers also use manuscript speeches when they want their exact words to be used. It is also the style employed by people who use TelePrompTers. This format also ensures exact adherence to a timetable, which can be essential when each speaker is alotted a specific amount of time.

Because listening to a speech being read can be dull for the audience, it is essential to have copies of your speech for handouts. You can use visual aids with a manuscript speech to help make it more interesting for the audience.

Unless you have to use the manuscript style, it is best to avoid it. If you have material that has to be presented exactly as written, do so, but try to paraphrase the rest of the speech. If you must read from a manuscript, use the scope technique—slide your thumb and index finger down the page, scoping one section at a time. This will help you to find your place after you look up at the audience. Manuscript presentations require a great deal of practice to be done well.

5. MEMORIZED STYLE

Unless you are a professional actor who can memorize speeches and make them sound like you just came up with them, forget about memorized style presentations. Most people cannot memorize every word they have written. And spoken language and written words have obvious differences. People are not accustomed to hearing the written word used in speech. Oral language consists of short sentences and phrases, contractions, slang, and starts and stops. Written language consists of longer, more formal sentences with transitions. It looks OK on paper, but it doesn't sound so good when you speak it.

The most painful public speaker to watch is one who has written a speech, thinks he or she has it memorized, gets up to the podium, and forgets it. Because of the way the presentation has been prepared, he or she is unable to go on or even to come up with an alternative opening line. There is little chance of success with a memorized speech. As a speaker, you depend on cues from listeners to guide your delivery, adapting it when necessary to meet their needs. You will not be able to do this with a memorized presentation, and you will be leaving yourself open to failure.

Figure 10.1 summarizes the five styles of delivery that have been discussed in detail in this chapter and when to use them.

Figure 10.1

THE FIVE STYLES OF DELIVERY AND WHEN TO USE THEM

Style	Description	When to Use It
Impromptu	Off the cuff	Spur of the moment
Extemporaneous	Planned, prepared, practiced	Planned events
Expromptu	Prepared	Meetings, short notice, not practiced
Manuscript	Written and read word-for-word	Scientific and political conferences
Memorized	Recited word-for-word	Never!

11 Delivery Techniques: The Three Vs

The way you deliver your message to other people is made up of three components, the *three Vs*: *visual, vocal,* and *verbal.* Each carries a portion of the total message. The *visual* is what we look at: dress, body language, posture, and facial expression. The *vocal* is your voice and how it sounds to others. The *verbal* is the words you choose. These three components are far from equally weighted. Since visual has the most impact (55 percent), it is important that you as a presenter properly prepare yourself to show your audience a positive visual message.

THE VISUAL

Dress for Success

How you look can color what people hear you saying. If you have done your homework and researched the audience, you can choose clothing that will enhance your presentation and be appropriate for the occasion. For men, a suit demonstrates more authority than does a sportscoat or blazer. However, if you are in a warm-weather climate and many members of the audience are wearing short-sleeve shirts or dressing more casually, a suit may make you seem standoffish. When unsure of what to wear, ask the person who has scheduled you to present, or talk to others in the company.

For men, dark colors such as navy blue, gray, and black communicate power and authority. For big men, black may seem too austere. Keeping the suit jacket closed gives the impression of a broad chest and narrow waist. White or light blue shirts are always appropriate, along with silk ties, high-rise socks, and polished, dark leather shoes.

Many companies have business casual days. As an outside visitor to the firm, this does not apply to you unless you are requested to wear business casual attire.

Figure 11.1 outlines appropriate traditional business and business casual wardrobes for men.

Women do not have to dress like men to appear professional. Skirts should not be too short or too tight. Check to see that there are no runs in your stockings and carry an extra pair for emergency. Shoes should be conservative with low to mid heels. Jewelry should not clang or dangle. Sweaters should not cling and blouses should not be low cut. Find out which colors look best on you and wear them. If you are unsure, a professional image or color consultant is a worthwhile person to consult. Make sure your clothes fit properly.

Figure 11.2 outlines appropriate traditional business and business casual wardrobes for women.

If you wear glasses, save the tinted lenses for weekends. People want to see your eyes when you speak. The day of your presentation is not the time for new shoes, unless you have broken them in first. You don't want to find yourself standing in front of a group with a pained expression because your feet hurt. If you are unsure as to how your clothing looks, have someone view you from all sides—including the rear. Clothing that fits poorly will distract from what you have to say. Audience members may remember your split seam instead of the speech.

Figure 11.3 is a checklist of grooming guidelines for both men and women.

Figure 11.1

WARDROBES FOR MEN

Basic Traditional Business Wardrobe

- Two-piece suits. Several two-button, three-button, or double-breasted suits in navy, gray, charcoal, or pinstripes. Avoid brown. Double-breasted jackets must be buttoned except when sitting down. Suit jackets should not be worn with other trousers.
- Sportscoats and trousers should contrast for a more casual look.
- Ties should be silk or wool. Color and patterns should not be loud or flashy. Burgundy, red, and navy work as background colors. Small prints and stripes are good choices. Paisleys are good alternatives. Do not wear a matching handkerchief. Knot should fill the space at the shirt top.
- Shirts should be long-sleeved, even in warm weather. Solid colors are preferred. Shirts should be well pressed. Avoid lavender, peach, plaids, dots, and broad stripes.
- Polished leather shoes in a dark color (black is best).

Business Casual Wardrobe

- Chinos or khaki-type trousers
- Sports shirts with collars or banded necks
- Polo shirts with collars
- Sweater or sports jacket
- Casual loafers or lace-up shoes

Always check the backdrop color for large presentations. Neither men nor women want to blend in and disappear. Figure 11.4 lists five questions to ask before you buy any garment for your wardrobe.

Figure 11.2

WARDROBES FOR WOMEN

Basic Traditional Business Wardrobe

- Black, navy, or gray two-piece suits.
- Contrasting jacket and skirt.
- Two-piece dress or dress with jacket.
- Several neutral blouses (white/off-white)
- Solid color blouse; may be pastel.
- One pair gold, one pair silver earrings.
- Scarves that pick up colors from suits or blouses.
- Black pumps; navy or taupe pumps.
- Neutral or taupe hosiery.

Business Casual Wardrobe

- Casual skirts or slacks. Neatly pressed chinos or corduroys are acceptable.
- Cotton shirts in solids, prints, or muted plaids.
- Sweaters (not too tight).
- Blazers to wear over slacks or skirts.
- Low-heeled shoes or boots.

Stand Up Straight! Posture Is Important

Many of us have been told since childhood to stand up straight, yet we're really not sure what to do. To evaluate your own posture, first look at yourself on video or in photographs. If you slouch and you don't like the way you look, give yourself these directions:

- My feet are hip width apart
- My arms are by my sides

Figure 11.3

GROOMING GUIDELINES

- Clean hair; if you spot dandruff flakes, use scotch tape to remove them before your presentation begins
- Clean, well-pressed, unspotted clothing
- Clean, clear glasses (no sunglasses indoors)
- No glasses hanging on chains or other devices
- Polished, clean, white teeth
- Good breath—avoid onion, garlic, dairy products
- Facial hair (and nose hair) trimmed for men, removed for women
- Check a full-length mirror

Figure 11.4

FIVE QUESTIONS TO ASK BEFORE YOU BUY

1. Does the garment fit? Check to see if it is too tight or too large. Don't buy "your size." Buy the size that fits today, not the size you hope to be.
2. Can you sit down without the buttons pulling in front?
3. Did you use a three-way mirror to check front, back, and side views?
4. Can you move and gesture easily?
5. Does it create the image you want?

- My shoulders are over my hips
- My neck is free
- My back is lengthening and widening
- My posture is good

When you are seated, you want to look energized and confident. You don't want to lean or slouch or appear too comfortable or relaxed. Proper seated posture when you are presenting (or just want to look good at a meeting) is sitting straight up in your chair, spine straight, with your feet flat on the floor.

Be Aware of Your Facial Expressions

Put a mirror next to your desk at work for one week. Watch your face when you are talking on the telephone. Be aware of any artificial, unfriendly, or deadpan expressions you may be making. Do you squint, frown, make strange faces? Once you become aware of the expressions you make, it will be easier for you to eliminate them. Practice smiling and looking pleasant. That's how you want to look during your presentation.

Gestures Are Part of the Visual Picture

Gestures are heightened conversation. They are visual reinforcements of the words and ideas you are trying to communicate to your audience. Gestures include hand, arm, and head movements and can enhance your presentation or detract from it. Have you ever had a conversation with someone who "talks with their hands"? In some cultures, it is an accepted and commonplace addition to spoken communication. In our culture, some hand gestures, such as finger pointing and fist raising, can be interpreted as hostile or threatening.

When giving presentations, men frequently stand in the "at ease" position commonly used in the military. They cross their hands behind their backs, and they keep them there. Or they cross their hands low in front of them like a fig leaf on a statue. Both men and women frequently cross their arms over their chests, thinking that they appear relaxed and confident. To many in the audience, this stance makes the speaker look defensive. By facing the audience with your arms crossed, you are closing yourself to it, and it will sense this. Since your objective is to communicate with openness and sincerity, you want to make open gestures to reinforce what you are saying.

Another gesture to avoid is putting your hands in your pockets. Some nervous presenters use this as a way of keeping their shaking hands out of sight and often wind up jingling the change or their keys without realizing it. Some people can't get their hands back out again and wind up spilling out the contents of their pockets as they try to release their hands. To avoid embarrassment, it's wise to empty your pockets of change and keys before presenting.

Clasping your hands into a folded position as when praying is still another gesture to eliminate. This gesture tightens you up and pulls in your energy instead of releasing it and allowing you to reach out to the audience. A weak twirling motion with your hands or wagging your fingers when making a point also indicates your unease to the audience.

Why Use Gestures?

When gestures are used in a positive way, they can warm both you and your audience. Used appropriately, they help you to relax during your presentation, just as stretching and other warm-up exercises helped you to relax your body before your presentation. Gestures also help you to emphasize important points during your presentation. They help back up what you are saying with a visual message.

The most effective gestures are spontaneous ones. They come from what you are thinking and feeling and they help the audience to relate to you and what you are telling them. It is much more effective to watch a speaker who uses movement than to listen to someone standing behind a lectern with hands clasped in front of him. Whose message will be remembered more?

Using Gestures Effectively

Have you ever watched an evangelist on television who used wide, sweeping gestures while speaking? These gestures are effective because they include everyone, making members of the audience feel a part of things even though they are simply watching from their own homes.

As a presenter in a business setting, you will be using gestures sparingly, and only to emphasize points in your presentation. But like the television evangelist, when you gesture, use the upper quadrant of your body, and make your gestures up and out to the audience. Your movements should be broad and flowing, not fast and jerky. The most effective gestures are natural extensions of yourself.

Your gestures should be varied; don't use the same motion over and over again. Repetition can be distracting to your audience and you may find that they are watching your gestures instead of listening to your presentation. Some gestures interfere with the audience's ability to pay attention, such as those threatening ones mentioned earlier (finger pointing and fist waving). Instead, use your palms and open them out to your audience. Move your arm and hand as a single unit, gesturing up and out toward the audience. Use either one or two arms. Try a sweeping motion and relate the extent of your gestures to the size of your audience. Bigger audiences need bigger gestures. Don't forget that nodding the head, smiling, and tilting the head to the side are all effective ways to emphasize what you are saying. As a presenter who uses gestures effectively, you will be projecting confidence and competence and the response you get from your audience will let you know when you have succeeded.

Listeners also feel more comfortable with a speaker who uses gestures effectively. Gestures work best when they are natural and spontaneous. Practiced gestures can look stiff and stilted when "performed" during a presentation. You can, however, learn how to gesture effectively.

12 Steps to Effective Gesturing

- Use gestures sparingly to emphasize major points.
- Let your movements be broad and flowing, not fast and jerky.
- Vary your gestures.
- Don't point your finger or your fist—these gestures are intimidating.
- Use your palms and open them to your audience.
- Move your arm and hand together as a single unit to avoid floppy wrists or elbows.
- Use large gestures for a large audience and narrow them for a smaller group.
- Evaluate your gestures by practicing in front of a mirror.
- Nods and smiles will make you seem confident to your audience.
- Avoid gestures that make you seem nervous or defensive. Don't stand with your hands behind your back or crossed in front of you.
- Don't keep your hands in your pockets.
- Keep hands and gestures above your waist.
- Gestures should be upward and open.

Skill Drill

Three times a week, for one minute each time, stand in front of a full-length mirror and practice gestures. When you are comfortable gesturing, use them with the five-minute persuasive speech you prepared previously. Videotape yourself, critique your gesturing skills, make any necessary adjustments.

THE VOCAL

Since a large portion of your presentation's memorability factor is vocal (38 percent), your voice and pitch matter. When we are stressed, our voices tend to rise, but the deeper the pitch of your voice, the longer people will listen to what you have to say. There is an exercise you can practice to gain control over your pitch and to bring it into a lower range. Repeat the following three sentences, each at a deeper pitch:

- "This is my normal pitch."
- "Do, Re, Me, Fa, So, La, Ti, Do"
- "This is my normal voice."

Stop and listen for a difference between the first and last sentences. Repeat the trio of sentences until you are in control of your pitch and can deepen it at will. Practice this exercise 10 times each day, and after six weeks you will have greater control over your pitch.

Volume

Even the most interesting presentation will fail if it can't be heard; conversely, if it is delivered in a very loud voice, it will fail as well. Being able to control your volume, and vary it, will help you hold the audience's attention. There are two exercises that can help you control your volume: Breathing from the diaphragm and speaking as if your voice is hitting the back wall. Breathing from the diaphragm allows more air flow and will help you avoid a sore throat.

Skill Drill

Ask someone to record the first few minutes of your presentation while carrying the tape recorder from the front to the back row. Keep practicing until the tape picks up your voice from the back row and you are comfortable projecting your voice.

Fast Talk/Slow Talk

The normal speaking rate is between 120 and 160 words per minute. If people are always asking you to repeat yourself, you probably talk too fast. If they often interrupt you, you probably speak too slowly. To control your rate, read aloud. Take 160 words from any source and time yourself as you read them. You will then know whether to slow down or speed up your normal rate. Practice every day until comfortable with your new rate of speech.

Voice Problems

Your voice becomes a problem when it calls attention to itself. There are several common voice problems:

- **Harshness**—Unless it is physical in origin, a harsh voice indicates tension and stress. Use relaxation techniques to help eliminate the problem. If your throat is dry, drink warm water with lemon before speaking.
- **Nasality**—Nasality is frequently caused by speaking with the jaws clenched. It can be reduced by opening the mouth wider and using the tongue more firmly.

- **Breathlessness**— Breathlessness is usually caused by insufficient breathing while speaking. Take deeper breaths and release a controlled flow of air.
- **High pitch**—Unless physical in origin, high pitch can be improved via vocal exercises and a conscious effort to speak in your lower vocal range.

Pauses and Power Robbers

We hear competent speakers every day. Listen to radio or television and you will hear confident, authoritative men and women telling us about the news, commenting on current events, or even endorsing products. How do these people sound and what kind of words do they use? Do they use jargon or buzz words? Professional speakers use clear, colorful language in short, simple sentences that everyone can understand.

All too often, our verbal skills distort our images as capable, knowledgeable professionals. We hem and haw, trying to find the right word. We may even discount ourselves and our ideas without realizing it, or we may unknowingly offend others with our language.

All of these verbal faults are "power robbers" that detract from our confidence, authority, professionalism, and power. Hedges and qualifiers are also common power robbers. These are the filler words we use when we are uncertain about what we have to say or are uncomfortable with silence. The *ums, ahs, likes,* and *you knows* that have no place in a sentence become distracting and annoying if they are abundant.

I recently went to hear a psychologist speak. She had an interesting topic and was a very attractive presenter. Unfortunately, she had a very annoying habit that detracted from her interesting presentation—after the first five minutes of her presentation, I found myself counting the *um*s in her speech. I stopped counting at 100.

Another common power robber is the pause that is misused. An effective pause emphasizes what has just been said or what is to come. For example, if you are going to announce a decision you have made or a new product your company is coming out with, your speech should have pauses for dramatic emphasis: "Our company, a leader in the synthetic fur industry, will be bringing to the market a product so realistic, there has never been anything like it before. Our new creation is called (pause)—minkella." This brief pause sets the listeners up to hear the announcement of a new product called minkella. Even if they were only half listening before, when the speaker pauses, he or she recaptures their attention. They want to know what's coming after the pause.

On the other hand, there are some pauses that can hurt your presentation—pauses that detract from what you are trying to say because they come at inappropriate times during your presentation, for instance, when you have forgotten what you wanted to say or have lost your place.

Tag questions can have the same effect. These are questions at the end of a sentence that give the impression that we are unsure of what was just said or are looking for approval: "I believe my group's solution to the problem of wasteful spending is a good one, don't you?" The "don't you" gives that strong declarative sentence a weak ending. Think about what you really want to say and how you are going to say it. Then say exactly what you mean.

Passive sentences are also power robbers. Active sentences show that we took the initiative and performed an action. Passive sentences and words say that things happened to us or around us. For example, consider "I hit the ball" (active) versus "the ball was hit by me" (passive). Active words give us more power. Consider also "Due to increased client demand, I was forced to develop my organizational and writing skills." A more powerful, active way to say this is "I developed my organizational skills and sharpened my professional writing abilities to better service growing client demands." This highlights your initiative and effort in the situation in a positive way.

Two of the most powerful words in the English language are *you* and *I*. The word *you* is most effective when influencing, persuading, or selling to someone. The focus should be on the people we are speaking to. After all, they're not going to do something just because you think it's a good idea. They're going to respond to what they think, feel, and want. Most of our statements in business should be *you*-based: "*You*'re going to love this new copy machine. Imagine all the benefits to *you* and *your* company."

The word *I* is best used in a conflict situation. When we are in conflict, we often begin by accusing and attacking the other person: "You were wrong. You made a mistake. You made me look bad." The other person, upon hearing this tirade of *you*s, begins to withdraw or to become defensive. Either way, the communication is stopped because he or she is no longer listening to you. A more effective way to approach conflicts is to use the word *I*: "I feel that there was a mistake made. I was embarrassed and felt that we could have been better prepared." Nothing in that statement is directly accusing, yet you are still getting your message across and chances are that the other person is still listening.

The idea behind understanding which words send which messages is to make conscious decisions about the words you choose. Instead of saying things out of habit, be aware of what you say and create new, more effective habits when you speak.

You can work to minimize the effect of power robbers on your speaking habits in three ways:

- by identifying your own tendencies
- by correcting the behavior

- by practicing to replace the bad habit with a good one permanently

Proper Grammar and Diction

The way you pronounce words can be a big factor in your ability to influence people. Even the best-prepared, -researched, -written, and -practiced presentation will fail if you mispronounce words, use them incorrectly, or use poor diction. People who mispronounce words are thought to be poorly educated or not very bright. This is frequently untrue. Many mispronunciation problems are the result of bad diction habits, of regional peculiarities, or of knowing the word from having read it but never having heard it spoken. President Jimmy Carter, who certainly knew the word, always spoke the word *nuclear* as "nucular," a common error in pronunciation. I don't know if it was brought to his attention and he couldn't correct it or if he felt he was using the correct pronunciation. Most pronunciation and diction problems can be corrected by listening to good speakers, by asking when you are not sure how to pronounce a word, or by getting coaching from a qualified speech instructor.

Emphasis

When we speak, we tend to emphasize certain words or phrases. In your presentations, the words and phrases you emphasize should be ones that will bring home your point to the audience. You can change the meaning of a sentence simply by changing which words you emphasize. The technique used to emphasize words or phrases in your presentation is called "punching it." Professional speakers and speech writers underline the words and phrases they want to emphasize. You can do the same on your own outline, and when you practice the presentation, practice punching it as well. For example, in this sentence, change in the emphasis changes the speaker's intent: "When we deal with companies your size . . ." versus "When we deal with companies your size . . . "

Skill Drills

#1: Read both of the phrases above out loud, putting the emphasis on the underlined word. The emphasis on the word *your* in the first phrase makes the company sound small, possibly insignificant. When you read the second phrase, putting the emphasis on the word *size,* the listener will feel that you are impressed by the size of his or her company.

#2: Read aloud and tape record yourself; use emphasis when reading. Reading children's books aloud works well. Concentrate on your voice projection, diction, and tempo. Do this exercise three times a week, 10 minutes per session.

Finish with Strength

Does your voice tend to rise at the end of a sentence? Tape record yourself speaking the first few lines of your presentation. If your voice goes up at the end of a sentence, it will sound as though you are asking a question or are tentative about what you just said. If you tend to swallow your last few words, that will reduce the impact of what you are saying as well. Finish sentences completely and drop your pitch slightly while keeping the volume strong. Listen to newscasters as they close their broadcasts; most of them use a tag line which they repeat regularly with volume up and pitch down. Practice until comfortable with the way you sound.

THE VERBAL

It may be difficult to accept that after all the hard work and preparation that goes into a presentation, the verbal message or content accounts for the smallest portion of the impact on most audiences. Obviously, what you have to say is important, and communicating your ideas clearly and concisely will be your greatest challenge as a presenter. Your audience will be looking for "WIIFM" from the moment you begin to speak. Make sure that your opening sentences tell them what they can expect to get from your presentation.

One key to audience acceptance and respect is to look, talk, and act the way your audience does. That does not mean dressing casually or sloppily if you are addressing a group of college students, but it does mean that you should keep the audience in mind when writing your presentation so you can use familiar words and concepts that will be of interest to them. Consider using anecdotes to bring yourself into the world of your listeners by relating experiences you may have in common with them. If your presentation is to a technical group, by all means use technical terms and jargon, but using more colorful language as well could make your presentation more interesting.

For all presentations, use simple, descriptive language. Adjust your vocabulary to suit the group. The more you know about who your listeners are, the easier it will be for you to speak their language. Avoid foreign phrases unless you plan to translate them for the audience. Keep your sentences and words short. What words can you eliminate to make your speech more concise? If you are using language that can mean different things to different members of the audience, be sure to explain your meaning. For example, *politics* can refer to a system or government or to the inner dynamics of an organization. There is a world of difference between saying that a product is "cheap" and saying that it is "inexpensive."

Be sure that you have taken the audience's industry or profession into account when preparing your presentation. Be sincere and don't ever pretend that you have things in common with your audience when you don't. Be honest. Your words will paint a picture for your listeners, and using colorful and descriptive language will help you bring it to life for them.

Visual, Vocal, Verbal Checklist

Visual

- Dress appropriately to help, not hinder, your presentation.
- Step out from behind the lectern.
- Speak with confidence and authority.
- Smile.
- Get set before starting to speak.
- Establish eye contact with your audience before speaking.
- Begin speaking without looking at your notes.
- Refer to your outline only occasionally.
- Don't look at the floor or out the window.
- Use gestures effectively (open palms, vary motions; keep them visible, smooth, natural).
- Stand up straight yet relaxed; don't lean.
- Use your facial expressions to add interest—look confident.
- Keep your chin up.
- Keep your feet still (no dancing, shifting, or crossing legs). Keep your movements intentional.
- Don't pace.

- Move about; leave the podium. Get closer to your audience.
- Look like you are enjoying yourself.
- Use your body language to show you care that your audience listens.
- Appear confident and relaxed.
- Don't play with your pens, pointers, visuals, hair, or jewelry or rattle change in your pocket.
- Don't pack up to leave before the entire audience has left the room.

Vocal

- Speak with enthusiasm.
- Sound interested and sincere.
- Sound extemporaneous, not like you are reading or have memorized your presentation.
- Keep your pitch comfortably low; use variation in tone.
- Keep your speaking rate at 125 to 160 words per minute. Vary the rate.
- Pronounce your words carefully. Enunciate clearly.
- Avoid power robbers.
- Use pauses for impact.
- Use voice variation (pitch, volume, rate, punch).
- Stop at the end of an idea; don't hook sentences together with *and, and uh, like.*
- Drop your pitch, not volume, at the end of sentences.
- Don't let your voice rise at the end of declarative sentences.
- Hide, don't emphasize your mistakes.
- Speak with, not at, the audience.

Verbal

- Use descriptive language.
- Start with a grabber to get their interest and create need.
- Use transitions to make your ideas flow.
- Make sure your information is interesting, useful, and understandable.
- Repeat the information to enhance retention (without being redundant).
- Avoid words that create doubt about what you are saying (*kind of, sort of, I hope, I guess, perhaps*).
- Time your speech accurately.

Five Steps to Perfect Delivery

- Proper preparation should continue right up to the moment the presentation begins.
- Arrive early.
- Check all equipment.
- Check the room layout.
- Check the lighting.
- Get out your materials.
- Check your appearance.
- Put up your title visual.
- Distribute your handouts.

1. Deliver Your Presentation

Before you begin to address the audience, turn off any visuals that have been showing. This is done so the audience's attention is focused solely on you, the speaker. Remembering to breathe fully and deeply, take the platform, face the audience, make eye contact, and proceed with the introduction, grabber first. Movement begins only after the opening is finished.

2. Dealing with Interruptions

Interruptions can wreck even the best-planned presentation and many interruptions can be avoided by taking simple precautions ahead of time. These can include the following:

- Closing the doors to the presentation room
- Posting a sign warning that a presentation is in progress
- Posting an associate by the door
- Rerouting phones in the room
- Asking that questions and comments be held until the end of the presentation
- Letting the audience know that there will be a break and when it will be

3. What should you do if you get off track?

There is always the danger of departing from the planned outline and addressing subjects originally not intended as part of the presentation. Whether precipitated by an audience member's question or the speaker's desire to be as informative as possible, the result is often a loss of focus and a reduction in the presentation's effectiveness.

Getting off track can often be avoided by being aware of the danger ahead of time and making a conscious effort to avoid it. This effort should be one of the motivating factors in the development of a tight outline and a final draft that can be referred to easily during the presentation. You should only consider speaking without notes if you have been able to rehearse enough to have thoroughly learned the outline. During the presentation, only those audience questions relevant to the topic being covered should be addressed. With others, an offer can be made to get together with the questioner after the presentation for a discussion. Additional control can be exerted by asking, during the preview portion of the presentation's introduction, that the audience hold all questions until the end of the presentation. If, despite precautions, the presentation gets off track, the speaker should pause, use his or her notes to determine what was last covered, and then resume. If an audience member is involved, the speaker can offer to discuss the matter later while also explaining the need to get the presentation back on track for the benefit of everyone attending. If the presenter's superior is involved, he or she can be asked if the new subject should be further explored or if the presentation should return to what was originally planned. This last tactic most often elicits, without confrontation, a directive to return to the original presentation content.

4. A Second Closing Statement

A second closing statement is needed if questions have followed the presentation. The all-too-common indecisive ending, often consisting of a mumbled reference to the lack of more questions or time, should be avoided at all costs. You now have another opportunity to reinforce your main points and make a memorable statement.

5. Getting Feedback

Getting feedback from both audience members and unbiased sources will help you to improve your presentation skills. When appropriate, evaluation forms can be distributed; when not, follow-up calls to audience members can be helpful. Unobtrusive tape recorders and video cameras can be particularly helpful by showing the speaker what the audience experienced. Figure 11.5 is an example of a presentation feedback evaluation form.

Figure 11.5

PRESENTATION FEEDBACK EVALUATION FORM

Presentation: ____

Presenter: __________________________ Date: ____________________

Your comments and observations are highly valued. Please take a few minutes to answer the following questions:

What is your overall evaluation of the presentation? Check the appropriate box.

☐ Unsatisfactory ☐ Marginal ☐ Good ☐ Very Good ☐ Excellent

Was the purpose of the presentation clearly communicated?

What, if any, difficulty did you have following the presentation?

What concepts, if any, should have been explained better?

What about the presentation did you find most valuable/beneficial?

What about the presentation did you find least valuable/beneficial?

What would you say were the presenter's strengths?

What would you suggest the presenter improve?

General comments:

WHAT TO DO WHEN YOU HAVE TO CUT YOUR PRESENTATION

You're ready with your presentation, but unfortunately you are last on the day's agenda and the other speakers went long. The moderator has just told you that instead of having 60 minutes to present, you will have only 5 to 10 minutes. Don't panic. You can cut your speech successfully without losing too much impact if you follow these guidelines:

- Pick one key point to focus on.
- Use a strong grabber, such as, "Forty percent of today's teenagers are being brought up in single parent homes. And teenagers committed 40 percent of all violent crimes."
- Give a strong follow-up to your grabber, such as, "By the time today's teens become parents, 60 percent of their children will be living with only one parent. And teenage crime will be up another 30 percent."
- Illustrate your point with an anecdote or story so the point is driven home to the audience.
- To structure your shortened speech effectively, use the following format:
  1. State the problem.
  2. State your solution.
  3. Tell how or why you reached your solution.
  4. Sum up.

12 Platform Dynamics

POSTURE AND MOVEMENT

Have you ever watched a speaker sway or rock at the podium? It's very distracting and can detract from even the most interesting speech. How you appear to your listeners will have an impact on their reaction to what you are going to tell them. Your posture and the way you conduct yourself on the platform is an important part of your presentation. Your objective is to be comfortable and controlled while you are presenting. You want the audience to see that you are relaxed and in control.

To achieve a comfortable speaking position, stand up and spread your feet about six to eight inches apart, parallel to each other with toes pointed straight ahead. Flex your knees and put your weight on the balls of your feet. Standing in this position will stop any swaying or rocking motion and will diminish any distracting heel movements.

Comfortable movements will relax both you and your audience. Take at least two steps, and then get back into position. Do not pace; it's distracting. Use movements to establish contact with your audience. You may even want to walk to the side or rear of the room, pause there, speak, and then return to your place in front. Getting physically closer to your audience increases its attention and interest. It also encourages response if you are asking questions. The accepted public distance zone is 12 to 25 feet. In smaller group situations, you can approach within a social distance of 4 to 12 feet primarily and occasionally get as close as 18 inches to 4 feet.

Stand up straight and face the audience head-on. Keep your posture open with arms relaxed and hanging down at your sides. If your arms are crossed in front, it may make you seem defensive. Hold your head up high with your chin up. Having your chin raised gives you the aura of being in control; chin down connotes acquiescence. Visual signals that make you appear not to be in control will detract from your presentation.

THE EYES HAVE IT

Don't be afraid to make eye contact with your listeners; their reactions to you will help your performance as a presenter. If you sense boredom, you may have to pick up the pace; if you sense enthusiasm, it can help to pump you up. When you make eye contact, you are relating to your audience, which will help get your message across.

In order to make proper eye contact, think of the audience as sitting in a Z formation. Start with a familiar or friendly face. Look at that person for three to five seconds, or long enough to complete a thought, and then move on in a Z around the room. Break your Z by starting from the middle or the back of the room to vary your eye contact. If you make eye contact with someone who quickly turns away, try not to look directly into that person's eyes again. In some cultures, direct eye contact is inappropriate, and some people just feel uncomfortable being looked at. You may also nod occasionally, and you will probably get a nod back, at least if the person agrees with what you just said. If you get a head shake, you'll know who disagrees with you.

FACIAL EXPRESSIONS

It isn't easy to speak and smile at the same time, but it is important to smile during your presentation if congruent with your message. Some men find it more difficult to smile while presenting than women do, but practice helps here. Videotape your presentation or practice in front of a friend. Watch your expression and see if you have smiled enough and in appropriate places. If not, you can write reminder notes to yourself in the margin of your speech or just practice smiling beforehand.

BODY LANGUAGE

You're at a meeting and have just been asked for your views. You are unprepared and nervous and want to slump down in your seat so no one will notice you. No matter how nervous you are, now is the time to sit up straight in your chair, keep your hands above the table, use gestures, and make eye contact. While you are trying to collect your thoughts, open by paraphrasing the question you have just been asked. This will give you a brief amount of time to think of something to say. Others at the meeting will be responding to your body language. How you look, gesture, and make eye contact will be influencing the opinion of others at the meeting. You usually don't get a second chance to make a first impression, so the visual message you send must be strong and positive.

13 Stage Fright

You are comfortable with the visual, vocal, and verbal parts of your presentation. You have prepared properly and practiced perfectly. But you have a problem. You are nervous about presenting. You are not alone. Whether this is your first presentation, or your one hundred and first, almost everyone fears speaking in public. Actors suffer from the same feelings, and many say they never get over them. What they have learned, and what you can learn, is to take those feelings and use them to your advantage.

Although the fear of speaking in public ranks in public surveys ahead of fear of death, flying, heights, and snakes, this fear can be controlled. Performance anxiety is a normal feeling. And it is a form of energy that can be channeled to serve you well. To use these feelings to your own advantage, you must first identify them. There are four common fears that most speakers have:

1. **Fear of fainting.** Unless you have a medical problem, this is almost unheard of. You may feel faint, but it is highly unlikely that you will.
2. **Fear of being boring.** If you approach speaking as an audience-centered sport, you will seldom need to be concerned with boring your listeners. Make sure that
   - you are providing useful information
   - your material is interesting and you have backed it up with facts, figures, and anecdotes to enhance and illustrate your points

- you are speaking directly to each one of them so there is no reason for them to be bored
- you are enthusiastic about the topic and your voice shows it

3. **Fear of your mind going blank.** We have all seen this happen to other people, and you need to learn what to do if it happens to you. Pause, look at your notes or outline, and try to pick up again where you left off, or move on to your next thought. Don't be afraid to use your notes to get back on track. If you realize that you made a mistake during your presentation, correct it if it will have impact on the audience, or let it slide if it is insignificant.
4. **Fear of being judged.** If you are well prepared and have practiced enough, everything will go smoothly. It is important that the audience knows that you enjoy your subject, even if you've made some mistakes or have lost your place. A sincere presenter doing his or her best, who is obviously well prepared, will not be judged harshly.

Once you have identified your fears, begin work to manage them and let them help you.

First, accept that stage fright is a normal feeling, experienced by most people. Next, observe how other speakers handle their anxiety or ask them what they do to relax before a presentation. Perhaps you've noticed other speakers doing some breathing exercises or shoulder and head rolls before their presentations. Many speakers have brief exercise routines that help them relax. Others use self-talk to turn the fear into excitement. An important aspect of fear control is to speak frequently. As with any sport, the more you practice, the better you will become, and speaking is an audience-centered sport.

SELF-TALK BUILDS SELF-ESTEEM

The conversations you have with yourself build or destroy your self-image. If you can regulate your self-talk to upgrade your self-esteem, you can convince yourself of almost anything. If you walk into a presentation believing that you are going to fail, you probably will. But if you do as I do, and give yourself a positive self-talk, your chances for success will increase drastically.

I frequently use the self-talk mantra created by speech expert Dorothy Sarnoff. It goes like this: "I'm glad I'm here. I'm glad you're here. I care about you. I know that I know." The message you are sending to yourself is one of joy and ease. It expresses your pleasure in being there to present. It says, "I'm thinking about you." It energizes you as you show empathy for your listeners. And it communicates authority, that you have taken the time and effort to prepare a presentation worth giving and worth listening to.

Every time you arrive at a presentation, repeat this mantra to yourself over and over. Say it silently or out loud, fast or slow; it doesn't matter. It becomes a chant that lets you entertain only positive thoughts and messages. Positive self-talk is an effective means of controlling stage fright.

Another way to help you relax before your presentation is to try the simple exercise routine that I use before I speak. It can be done just about anywhere; I've even done it on an airplane!

BRODY'S BASICS

1. **The rag doll:** Stand up straight, feet comfortably apart. Stretch up tall, then bend over by collapsing quickly and loosely from the waist with your arms relaxed and hands dangling. Keep your arms, hands, and neck relaxed so you look like a rag doll. Do not bounce. Wait 10 seconds. Now slowly rise up to a straight position, keeping relaxed. Repeat five times.

2. **Head rolls:** Immediately after the rag doll, while your neck is still relaxed, stand straight with your hands close to your chest. Begin to slowly rotate your neck, first to the left, then forward with your chin down in front, then to the right. Don't roll your neck back. Reverse the rotation rolling to the right, then front, then left, then front. Be sure your neck is relaxed. Repeat five times.
3. **Arm swings:** After the head roll, stand straight with your arms to your sides. Swing your left arm in a large circle from front to back, as if you were doing the back stroke. Swing your right arm in a large circle from front to back in the same manner. Reverse and swing your left arm in a large circle from back to front. Do the same with your right arm. Swing your arms in this manner five times on each side.
4. **Shoulder shrugs:** Right after the arm swings, stand straight with your arms at your sides. Using your arms, move your shoulders straight up to the level of your ears. Drop your shoulders back down to their resting position. Shrug your shoulders four more times.
5. **Yawning:** After completing the rag doll and the head rolls, your face and neck muscles and vocal chords should be relaxed. Now, standing straight, slowly yawn, sounding an "ahhhhh" on exhalation. The sound you make is a relaxed sound. Strive for this relaxed and open quality whenever you speak.
6. **Abdominal breathing:** Sit upright in a chair and place both feet flat on the floor. Rest your hands in your lap. Take a deep breath through the nose while extending your stomach. Push your stomach out as the air comes into and fills your lungs. Your shoulders can rise and may possibly go back a bit. Place one hand on your chest and the other on your abdomen. Which hand rises most? If it is the hand on your abdomen, you are breathing properly. If not, pull your breath deeper into your lungs. Once your lungs are full, hold the air to the count of six and then let the air escape from your nose. Repeat, taking each deep breath slowly through the nose. Do this 10 times.

BRODY'S BASIC REFRESHERS

If you find you need a quick refresher before giving your presentation, here are two that you can do even while seated at your table or on the dais.

- **Deep Breathing I:** Take a deep breath in through your nose and tighten everything in your body, from your head, to your neck, shoulder, hands, fingers, legs, and toes. Hold the breath for 6 seconds, then slowly let go of the tension in your body as you exhale through your mouth to a count of 10.
- **Deep Breathing II:** Take a deep breath and clasp your hands together. Hold your breath as you squeeze your palms together tightly. Let go of your hands and breath at the same time.

Both of these deep breathing refreshers help you to slow your heartbeat. As you do this, you will also slow down the surge of adrenaline that is making you tense.

Tips for Handling Stage Fright

- Accept the fact that stage fright is normal; you may have it every time you speak, but let it work for you by thinking of it as excitement, not fear.
- Watch other speakers and learn their techniques.
- Concentrate on your strengths; compensate for your weaknesses.
- Practice, practice, practice before you are going to present. Remember, perfect practice makes perfect presentations.
- Speak often; the more you speak, the better you will be able to manage your stage fright.

Managing the Physical Symptoms of Stage Fright

For dry mouth:

- Take no milk products, soda, or alcoholic beverages.
- Eat no ice cream.
- Lightly coat your teeth with petroleum jelly ; it will stop your lip from sticking to your teeth.
- Bite the tip of your tongue (this helps you to salivate).
- Drink room temperature or warm water (with lemon, if available).

For sweaty hands/body:

- Use talcum powder or corn starch on hands/body.
- Carry a handkerchief.

If you have red splotches on your face:

- Wear pink or red colors.
- Wear high necklines.
- Use humor to release endorphins.

If your voice is shaky:

- Project your voice to the back row of the audience.

If your hands are shaky:

- Gesture; make them small gestures, don't wave about wildly.

If your legs are shaky or your knees are knocking:

- Move about the platform or walk.

If your heartbeat is rapid:

- Do some deep breathing.
- Avoid caffeine.

Getting Your Audience Involved

You've done your homework. Your PAL™ has been clearly identified and you are comfortable with your topic. But what of the listeners' expectations? What will they be expecting from you, and how can you improve your chances for a positive reaction from them?

Today's adult audiences expect a lot from a presenter. They've heard it all, seen it all, and their desire to be stimulated is fierce. They prefer not to sit and be lectured to; they want to be involved. When professional speakers were polled, more than 85 percent said they used some form of audience involvement. That is because audiences learn better and remember more when they are involved in your presentation. What can you as a presenter do to meet your audience's expectations?

- **Ask the audience questions.** These can be either real or rhetorical, and it's OK for you to answer them yourself. By asking a question, you have forced the audience to really listen to what you are saying. They won't know whether you expect an answer from them until your presentation continues. You are in control and have the ability either to answer the question yourself or to ask for an audience response. For example, ask, "What is the number one fear most adults have?" Now you can either give the answer yourself or take answers from the audience.
- **Get the audience to react or respond.** The easiest way to do this is to ask a question and request a show of

hands. For example, ask, "How many people in this room had pizza within the past two weeks?" This method will bring the audience's attention back to you if you sense you are losing it at any time during your presentation. It's a good idea for a speaker to have a list of questions that pertain to the presentation or that will stimulate the interest of the audience.

- **Tell the audience a story.** When listeners hear a well-told story, it becomes their story too or they relate your story to something that happened in their own lives or they may be reminded of a similar story that has meaning for them. If your story uses jokes or anecdotes, the laughter generated is also a form of audience involvement.
- **Use interactive activities.** This method can work even with large audiences. For example, say, "Turn to your neighbor and shake hands." Or, "Look at the person behind you. Now turn around and see if you can remember what color eyes he or she has." These activities, and others like them, make the audience feel more a part of your presentation than if it is just sitting and listening.
- **Have the audience participate in your presentation.** This method has been used to great success by magicians and sleight-of-hand artists for centuries. You can involve audience members in your own presentation by asking questions or by having them play games that make your point, do puzzles, play roles, or even demonstrate handshakes, as I do in one of my business etiquette presentations.
- **Use visual aids.** While your visual aid is being displayed, ask the audience a question or give it time to reflect on something you have said. For example, "When you look at this breakdown of ski resorts by state, isn't it true that Maine has relatively few for the number of mountains it has?"
- **Have the audience fill in the blanks.** During your presentation, refer to pages in the handout you have provided. Ask the audience to fill in sections you have left blank. For example, when talking about the 3 Vs, the Visual, Vocal, and Verbal, I leave out the percentage of relative impact each has. During my presentation, I ask the

audience which V they think has the highest percentage of impact. Then the next, and so on. Then I give them the correct answers and they are usually quite surprised to discover that the verbal portion of a presentation is worth only 7 percent.

- **Form small groups.** This method only works if the space and the timing allow for it. Break the audience into small groups and have them work together on a brief activity. For example: They can compile lists or rank previously provided items in order of importance. The activity should be brief and you should include the outcome in your presentation. For example, if the groups have compiled lists of reasons why PCs are better than Macs in an office environment, you should have a list already prepared. And if the group has answers other than the ones you are displaying, you should add them to your list. This works well with flipcharts and overheads or if you are using a computer display and have the equipment there to make additions to your existing work.
- **Use people's names.** This makes people feel more involved. In small group situations, talk directly to participants. For example, "Scott, when you gave your presentation, I was impressed by the way you made eye contact with everyone in the room." Or, "Rachel, when you and I met earlier today, you asked me a question about relaxation techniques."
- **Make direct eye contact.** This works with any audience size. When you speak and look directly into people's eyes, they feel that you are speaking directly to them. Of course, if they quickly look away from you, they may feel uncomfortable with direct eye contact, so don't look directly at them again. In some cultures, direct eye contact is either not looked upon favorably or is seen as a challenge, so if you are presenting in another country, check on the rules of etiquette there.
- **Move closer to the audience.** It will make listeners feel more involved. Get out from behind the podium, get off the stage, and walk among the audience. Some speakers are known for sitting at the edge of the stage, some for

walking up and down the aisles. Find something that works for you and works with your presentation. Try different approaches until you find ones that you are comfortable with. Even just walking on the stage can work.

WHY ISN'T ANYONE LISTENING?

If you have done a good job preparing your presentation and have included some audience involvement, you probably won't have justifiable complaints from the audience such as that your speech is hard to follow or that it's boring. And if you have checked the room carefully, it is unlikely that anyone will complain about being unable to hear you or see your visual aids. There are still times, however, when the unexpected can happen. Here are some situations you may find yourself in and how to handle them effectively:

- **An unexpected disturbance in the room, or just outside.** Unplanned and unexpected disturbances do happen. The extent of the distraction to the audience depends on how long the disturbance lasts and how you handle it. A loud noise, a baby crying, a relentless telephone can all cause you to lose your concentration and your audience to be distracted. You can make a joke to smooth things over and wait for the noise to end and the audience to resume paying attention to you; you can graciously announce that the parents of the crying baby are welcome to leave and return; you can disconnect or take the telephone off the hook (you should have taken care of this one before starting your presentation).
- **Movement in the room.** Sometimes people come in late or walk out during your presentation. Try to ignore this. Some comedians use this type of disturbance as part of their act; if you feel comfortable using humor, this can work for you. But for most presenters, it's best to just ignore the situation and continue with your presentation. If most of the audience starts to leave, take the hint and

end your presentation early. When you do your feedback follow-up, try to find out what went wrong.

- **Your memory fails.** Sometimes, in spite of all the hard work and practice you've done, you have a memory lapse. If you are comfortable with the material, just continue on as if nothing happened. Frequently your audience will have no idea that you have left something out. If it is obvious, however, this is a good time to make a joke. Using humor will put the audience at ease and give you a few moments to glance at your notes and regain your momentum.
- **A photographer is trying to take your picture.** Hold a pose for a few seconds during your presentation; this will give him or her the chance to photograph you in action.
- **There's a heckler in the audience.** I have never had this happen to me but I have been in audiences when it has. Let me reassure you that unless you are performing stand-up comedy, the chances of encountering a heckler are remote. However, if it should happen, do not respond to the taunts. If someone does not escort the heckler from the room or ask him or her to be quiet, simply sit down and only resume your presentation when the incident is over.

15 Questions and Answers

You have concluded your prepared presentation, but it isn't over yet. The question-and-answer period can make or break the audience's impression of you and your presentation. Do not try to escape this crucial time by sitting down or leaving the podium. This is an opportunity for you to shine and to clarify your ideas further. Do not give the audience the impression that you are relieved that your presentation is over and that all you want to do is leave the platform.

Dos and Don'ts for the Qs and As

Do

- let the audience know when you will be taking questions
- encourage the audience to ask questions
- listen carefully and rephrase questions before answering
- look at the questioner while rephrasing the question, but look at the audience while you are answering
- call on experts in the audience but take back control after they have responded
- set a time limit to control hostile questioners
- answer briefly but succinctly
- end the question-and-answer period with a closing remark

Don't

- let a stage hog take control
- treat a hostile questioner with hostility
- lie; if you don't know an answer, say so
- be long-winded

ENCOURAGING QUESTIONS

It is part of your job as presenter to encourage questions from the audience. In some groups, no one wants to raise a hand and go first, so you will have to make the first move. You can do this by saying, "A question I am usually asked is . . ." That should encourage others to speak up after you have answered your own question. Your position during this period should be closer to the audience. Step out from behind your lectern, even sit at the side of the stage if the audience will still be able to see you. Some speakers like to take questions while they stand amidst the audience. If the room set-up is appropriate and you feel comfortable, it is acceptable to run the question-and-answer period this way.

If people are not asking questions, it means that they are bored, are confused, are afraid to look or sound stupid, did not like your presentation, or want to leave. If after the first question no one else volunteers one, it is appropriate to wrap up your presentation with some final words. You can present another conclusion, return to your central theme, revert to your closing statement, or talk about next steps. Keep your remarks brief and end with a strong finish.

CONTROLLING QUESTIONS

As the presenter, it is up to you to control the question-and-answer periods. Your first decision is when you want to field questions. If you are giving a training session or a sales presentation, it probably makes sense to take questions during your presentation. This can be tricky and you must maintain control of the session. Don't get too far ahead of yourself. If someone asks a question that you will be covering later in your presentation, say so. You must also avoid a lengthy response to a question which may disturb your train of thought and the audience's ability to concentrate. You can also set aside question-and-answer periods at specified times during a presentation and announce them at the start of your program. This gives your audience the chance to formulate its questions during your presentation.

HANDLING THE HOSTILE QUESTIONER

As a presenter, you may find yourself facing a hostile questioner, and your skill at disarming verbal attacks will effect the presentation and your credibility with the audience. The following approach works to diffuse hostile questioners:

- Let them say whatever they want to say. You listen while they vent.
- Paraphrase what they have just said and how they feel about it without being condescending.
- Ask probing questions to try to find out what the real issues are.
- Choose one of the following options:
  - "I know what your issues are, now let me respond."
  - "Let's problem solve to work this out."
  - "Let's look into this together after this presentation has concluded."

By using this approach, you have indicated that you value the thoughts and feelings of the questioner. The audience will respect you, and you will diffuse the hostility at the same time.

HOW TO RESPOND TO QUESTIONS

When You Know the Answer

A good way to begin when you know the answer is to paraphrase the question or include it as part of the answer. This clarifies the fact that you do understand the question and have heard it correctly. Then answer it. Try to avoid the tendency to say, "That's a good question," before you answer or, "Did I answer your question?" after you have responded. When you compliment one questioner it becomes awkward if you don't compliment the next questioner, and so on. If you have asked, "Did I answer your question?" and the answer is negative, you have destroyed some of your credibility with the audience. A good way to make sure you have answered the question is to ask the same questioner if he or she has any other questions for you or would like more explanation.

When You Don't Know the Answer

When you don't know the answer to a question, be truthful. Simply say, "I'm sorry, I don't have the answer," and offer to get the information and get back to that person at a later time. You also can offer a source for the information, or you can open it up to the audience or an expert in the group who may know the answer. Don't dwell on it. Keep the question-and-answer session moving.

The Stage Hog

If you encounter a stage hog who persists in asking you one question after another, you will need to make a decision. If the questions are relevant to the topic and merit consideration, answer them, but after a few questions, nicely say that it's time to give someone else a turn. If the questions are not relevant, answer the first question or two and then cut him or her short. Acknowledge the questions, and request that he or she write the rest of them down, and offer to answer them after the presentation. Then move on to the next questioner. If you have identified a potential stage hog prior to your presentation, try meeting with him or her in advance to discuss his or her ideas. Mention any that have merit during your presentation; that will make the stage hog feel good and probably save you from disruption of your question-and-answer period.

Keys to a Successful Question-and-Answer Session

- Tell the audience when you will be taking questions and whether there is a limit on the number it can ask.
- Encourage questions with open body stance and personal enthusiasm; ask one yourself if necessary.
- Listen carefully and paraphrase questions before responding.
- Look at the questioner when rephrasing a question; look at the audience when responding.
- If you don't know the answer, say so. Offer to get back to the questioner either in writing or by phone at a later date.

- Don't let a stage hog take control.
- Handle hostile questioners with tact and diplomacy, but cut them short.
- Respect the questioner and don't be defensive.
- Keep your answers brief.
- End the question-and-answer session with a memorable closing statement.

CONCLUDE WITH A MEMORABLE STATEMENT

When your presentation is over and the questions have stopped, it's time to wrap up. This is not the time to issue a simple "thank you" and leave the podium. It's a chance for you to leave a lasting impression on the audience. Return to the central theme, revert to your closing statement, or talk about next steps. This shouldn't be a lengthy close, but it should wrap things up neatly. An example of a strong closing is, "We've learned how synthetic furs can be made to look and feel like real furs; now let's use this information to create the next generation of synthetics."

16 Evaluating Your Presentation

You've worked hard to deliver a polished and professional presentation. But it shouldn't just end there. After each presentation, take the time to evaluate your own performance. This is a real opportunity for you to learn from your mistakes and to give yourself a pat on the back for your accomplishments.

If it was appropriate, you will have given the audience a Feedback Evaluation Form (see page 137). Be sure to ask the audience to fill these out and to return them to you before leaving your presentation. Once the forms leave the room, chances are you won't get them back unless the person who organized the presentation collects them and sends them on to you.

After your presentation, do your own self-evaluation as well. Use the Self-Evaluation Form in Figure 16.1 on page 160 and grade yourself realistically on each of the 12 categories listed. Any grade below an A gives you an opportunity for improvement. Keep your self-evaluations and watch your progress as you continue to grow as a presenter.

MAJOR FAILINGS IN BUSINESS PRESENTATIONS

If your presentation did not live up to your expectations, it is as important for you to find out why as it is to understand what makes a presentation successful. Including a lot of information in your presentation, no matter how valuable, does not guarantee that it will be successful. In fact, sometimes the

Figure 16.1

SELF-EVALUATION FORM

Presenter: ______________________________

Presentation: ______________________ Date: __________

Category	Grade				
1. Opening statement	A	B	C	D	F
2. Voice and pitch	A	B	C	D	F
3. Delivery	A	B	C	D	F
4. Content	A	B	C	D	F
5. Gestures	A	B	C	D	F
6. Eye contact	A	B	C	D	F
7. Posture	A	B	C	D	F
8. Stage-fright control	A	B	C	D	F
9. Use of visuals	A	B	C	D	F
10. Audience rapport	A	B	C	D	F
11. Questions and answers	A	B	C	D	F
12. Closing remarks	A	B	C	D	F

amount of information presented can cause the overall failure of the presentation. Data dumps, prevalent in many technical presentations, can cause even those in the audience who are interested in the topic to start to drift away and focus their attention somewhere other than on the speaker. Here are some other reasons why presentations fail:

- The presenter isn't well prepared. You may think you know the topic so thoroughly that you can just get up and wing it. This is very risky. Unless this is an impromptu presentation, you should be doing a lot of research and advance preparation for your presentation. Even if you think you'll be able to cover everything, chances are once you are up in front of the audience, you will forget things you wanted to say. If you don't have to research the topic, you will still need an outline, an opening, and transitional phrases. Approach the topic from the audience's perspective. Your audience analysis will let you know whether or not it is familiar with your subject or if you will be educating it from scratch. If you have not prepared and practiced your presentation thoroughly, the audience will probably find out, and your presentation will not be as successful as it might have been had you taken the time necessary to do things right.
- A proper audience analysis has not been done. Knowing who is in the audience and what their motivation is can only help with creating an effective presentation. Presenting a speech on the benefits of investing in mutual funds to a group of displaced homemakers is bound to fail. Presenting general information to a group that is expecting complex technical data will also fall far short of audience expectations.
- The presenter is too dependent on notes. This may not seem like a serious obstacle to a good presentation, but the audience senses it when you don't know your topic cold. Reading notes might be acceptable when you have to present large lists or sets of figures but for these, using visual aids is more effective than reading. If you have to

read your speech because you haven't taken the time to practice it sufficiently, this will also be apparent to the audience and you will probably lose its attention at some point during your presentation.

- Leaving too many questions unanswered during your presentation tells the audience that you really don't know enough about the subject. If you have properly prepared your presentation, you will have achieved enough familiarity to answer many questions. If you can't, you have not prepared adequately. The audience does not expect you to know everything, but enough to impress it with your grasp of the subject matter.
- You are going on for too long. Don't ask an audience to sit for more than 30 to 45 minutes without giving it a break. Listeners will be unable to concentrate and you will lose their attention. If you are giving a lengthy presentation, break it up. If it is not practical for the audience to leave the room, at least have stretching breaks. Make sure you practice your presentation with the appropriate breaks so that you will have transitions to lead from one part of the presentation to the next.
- The room is not well set up. The back row can't see you; the side rows can't see your visuals; you can't see the audience on either side of you without craning your neck. If the room has fixed seating, you may be in trouble—walk around during your presentation to make sure everyone sees and hears you. If the room has moveable seating, make sure you arrive early enough to sit in each section and see if you can be seen clearly and if your visual aids can be seen. Have someone else sit in the back row and make sure you can be heard. Adjust the room accordingly before the audience arrives.
- Not ending with a strong call to action or drawing conclusions for the audience. Your presentation should not just stop with, "Thank you." This is your chance to end with a flourish. If you want the audience to take action, ask for it now. If you have points you want to make sure people remember, make them again now.

17 Presentation Preparation Review

Before making any presentation, use the following guides to make sure you haven't overlooked anything. They will help you to focus on the processes which will become more familiar the more you present.

Presentation Preparation Steps

1. State your purpose (inform, persuade, entertain).
2. Evaluate your audience (demographics, psychographics, attitudes).
3. Know the logistics.
4. Limit your topic.
5. Choose a method of organization.
6. Outline your main points.
7. Gather supporting data.
8. Write the introduction.
9. Write your outline.
10. Write your transitions.
11. Develop your conclusion.
12. Prepare sample questions (and answers).

Preparing A Final Draft

1. Use $8\frac{1}{2}$-by-11-inch paper, not index cards.
2. Write on only the top two thirds of the page.
3. Decide where to use visual aids; make notes in the margins of your draft.
4. Color code your presentation: could know, should know, must know.

Constructing a Visual Aid

1. Make it twice as large as seems necessary.
2. Use two or more to create interest.
3. Make sure visuals are simple, clear, and easy to see.
4. Use printed letters rather than script.
5. Print or draw with dark, heavy lines.
6. Use color to create impact, but no more than five colors.
7. Offer one key point per visual aid.
8. Write in upper and lower case or all lower case.
9. Check spelling carefully.
10. Practice using visuals before presenting.

Practice Techniques

1. Practice out loud, three to six times.
2. Practice where you will be speaking, if possible.
3. Practice with your visual aids.
4. Videotape your presentation, watch it, and make any necessary adjustments.

10 Rules of Effective Business Presentations

1. Keep it short. Most business presentations go on for too long and lose the attention of the audience. Remember, everyone there has something else to do that's urgent!
2. Know who is in the audience; that way you will not talk down to them or go over their heads.
3. Use visual aids to add interest.
4. Get the audience involved.
5. Start on time; end on time.
6. Dress appropriately in business attire, even if the audience does not.
7. Use short sentences and simple phrases.
8. Avoid humor unless you know it will be appreciated.
9. Distribute your handouts at the end of the presentation to avoid having the audience reading while you are speaking.
10. If you don't know the answer to a question, don't try to bluff. Say you don't know and offer to find out.

PREPARING WHEN THERE IS NO TIME TO PREPARE

You've just been called to make a presentation and you have one hour to prepare. After you panic, take a step back and evaluate the situation. You were called because you have either the knowledge, the experience, the insight, or the credentials to be of value to the group. The following steps will help you get through the last-minute presentation crisis:

1. Do a very quick PAL™. What's the purpose of your presentation? Who's going to be in the audience? Where is it going to be held?
2. Write your opening with grabber and 30 to 50 words in which you capture their attention while introducing your topic.
3. Outline the content. Limit yourself to one to three main points. Give examples for support. Write transitions between the key points.
4. Write your closing 30 to 50 words, in which you summarize your points and have a closing grabber or a call to action.
5. Practice your opening and closing. Write down any possible questions you can think of. Practice your opening and closing again until you know it.
6. Practice again.

PRACTICE TECHNIQUES

While preparing your presentation, you've become an expert on your topic. Each time you give a presentation, you will prepare an outline and use it to practice the presentation over and over again. Here are some practice methods to try.

- Practice your presentation differently each time you do it. If you practice it the same each time, you destroy any freshness or spontaneity in your delivery.
- If your presentation is complicated or technical, practice it to a spouse or friend who is most like your intended audience to gauge how easy the material is to understand.
- After practicing several times, try practicing just the rough spots. Try those along with your opening and closing statements, key points, and transitions until you are comfortable with them.
- Practice in the same way you will be presenting. If you will be standing, stand. If you will be seated, sit. Tape record yourself after you have practiced out loud several

times. As you listen, ask yourself if you would enjoy this presentation if you were a member of your audience. If you wouldn't, it's time to rewrite and practice again.

- Practicing in your head isn't practicing. We are all quite eloquent in our minds. However, when we speak out loud, something entirely different comes out. The only way to practice correctly is to practice out loud.
- Practice with your visual aids. During your last few practice sessions, use whatever aids or handouts you will be using during your presentation. This serves as a final check of whether you have too many visuals or not enough. There is still time for you to change things and make final adjustments.
- Do a dress rehearsal. Set up an area with a similar seating arrangement. Wear the clothes you plan to wear to the presentation. If possible, try to have a live audience. Give your entire presentation, including taking questions from the audience. Ask for feedback and make any last-minute corrections.
- Use every opportunity to practice. A perfect time is when you are driving in the car. You can speak out loud and play audio tapes you have made of your practice sessions. It is a perfect, quiet time to practice without using notes—perfect for preparing an impromptu presentation.

On Presentation Day

1. Arrive early and check the room.
2. Have telephone calls rerouted or unplug the phone.
3. Locate restrooms.
4. Have handouts ready; be sure to bring extras.
5. Check seating and rearrange it if necessary.
6. Test your equipment and make sure your visual aids can be seen from every seat.

7. Make sure you can be heard from the back of the room.
8. Set up your visual aids; tape wires down if needed.
9. Do body warm-ups, stretches, and relaxation exercises.
10. Check your appearance; make any necessary adjustments.

Conclusion

FINAL WORDS

You will be making different kinds of presentations throughout your business life. You will attend meetings, go on job interviews, possibly make sales calls, and speak at special occasions. Whether you are presenting alone or as part of a team, you will be judged on your performance—not just on what you have to say but on how you say it and how you look. As you become more comfortable making business presentations, you will continue to improve your techniques and become a more polished presenter. As your skills grow, keep the following in mind:

- Present as often as you can.
- Read as much as you can to strengthen your vocabulary.
- Observe other speakers and learn from them (their good points and their mistakes).
- Be on the lookout for stories and anecdotes to add interest to your presentation; keep a notepad handy to jot them down.
- Use a dictionary and thesaurus to add interest to your vocabulary.
- Practice your presentations with a tape recorder and do self-evaluations.
- Don't be discouraged; you can acquire the skills needed to be a good presenter.

Bibliography

Maggie Bedrosian, *Speak Like a Pro* (Rockville, MD: BCI, 1994).

Bob Boylan, *What's Your Point?* (New York: Warner, 1988).

Marjorie Brody, CSP, and Shawn Kent, *Power Presentations* (New York: John Wiley & Sons, 1993).

Ron Hoff, *I Can See You Naked* (Kansas City: Andrews and McMeel, 1988).

Clark Lambert, *The Business Presentations Workbook* (Englewood Cliffs, NJ: Prentice Hall, 1989).

Thomas Leech, *How to Prepare, Stage, & Deliver Winning Presentations* (New York: Amacom, 1993).

Paul LeRoux, *Selling to a Group* (New York: Harper & Row, 1984).

Stephen R. Maloney, *Talk Your Way to the Top* (Englewood Cliffs, NJ: Prentice Hall, 1992).

Myles Martel, *The Persuasive Edge* (New York: Fawcett Columbine, 1989).

Robert Nelson and Jennifer Wallick,*The Presentation Primer* (Burr Ridge, IL: Irwin, 1994).

John W. Osborne, *Talking Your Way to the Top* (San Marcos, CA: Avant, 1990).

Dorothy Sarnoff, *Never Be Nervous Again* (New York: Ivy, 1987).

Claudyne Wilder, *The Presentations Kit* (New York: John Wiley & Sons, 1990).

About Toastmasters International

If the thought of public speaking is enough to stop you dead in your tracks, it may have the same effect on your career.

While surveys report that public speaking is one of people's most dreaded fears, the fact remains that the inability to effectively deliver a clear thought in front of others can spell doom for professional progress. The person with strong communication skills has a clear advantage over tongue-tied colleagues—especially in a competitive job market.

Toastmasters International, a nonprofit educational organization, helps people conquer their pre-speech jitters. From one club started in Santa Ana, California, in 1924, the organization now has more than 170,000 members in 8,300 clubs in 62 countries.

How Does It Work?

A Toastmasters club is a "learn by doing" workshop in which men and women hone their communication and leadership skills in a friendly, supportive atmosphere. A typical club has 20 members who meet weekly or biweekly to practice public speaking techniques. Members, who pay approximately $35 in dues twice a year, learn by progressing through a series of 10 speaking assignments and being evaluated on their performance by their fellow club members. When finished with the basic speech manual, members can select from among 14 advanced programs that are geared toward specific career needs. Members also have the opportunity to develop and practice leadership skills by working in the High Performance Leadership Program.

Besides taking turns to deliver prepared speeches and evaluate those of other members, Toastmasters give impromptu talks on assigned topics, usually related to current events. They also develop listening skills, conduct meetings, learn parliamentary procedure and gain leadership experience by serving as club officers. But most importantly, they develop self-confidence from accomplishing what many once thought impossible.

The benefits of Toastmasters' proven and simple learning formula has not been lost on the thousands of corporations that sponsor in-house Toastmasters clubs as cost-efficient means of satisfying their employees' needs for communication training. Toastmasters clubs can be found in the U.S. Senate and the House of Representatives, as well as in a variety of community organizations, prisons, universities, hospitals, military bases, and churches.

How to Get Started

Most cities in North America have several Toastmasters clubs that meet at different times and locations during the week. If you are interested in forming or joining a club, call (714) 858-8255. For a listing of local clubs, call (800) WE-SPEAK, or write Toastmasters International, PO Box 9052, Mission Viejo, California 92690, USA. You can also visit our website at http://www.toastmasters.org.

As the leading organization devoted to teaching public speaking skills, we are devoted to helping you become more effective in your career and daily life.

Terrence J. McCann
Executive Director, Toastmasters International